BREAKUP RECOVERY 101

How to Heal from Heartbreak and Move Forward with Your Life

Nora Williams

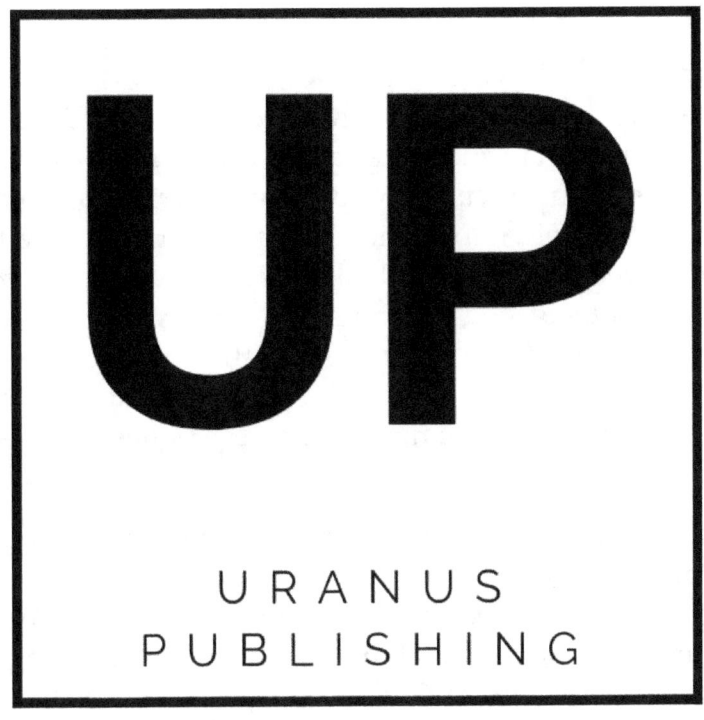

All rights reserved © 2021 by Nora Williams

...

ISBN: 978-1-915218-00-1
First Edition: October 2021

This book is copyright protected. It is only for personal use. You cannot amend, distribute, sell, use, quote, or paraphrase any part of this book's content without the author or publisher's consent. All pictures contained in this book come from the author's personal archive or copyright-free stock websites (Pixabay, Pexel, Freepix, Unsplash, StockSnap, etc.).

Disclaimer Notice:

Please note the information contained within this document is for educational and entertainment purposes only. All effort has been executed to present accurate, up-to-date, reliable, complete information. No warranties of any kind are declared or implied. Readers acknowledge that the author is not engaged in rendering legal, financial, medical or professional advice. The content within this book has been derived from various sources. Please consult a licensed professional before attempting any techniques outlined in this book.

By reading this document, the reader agrees that under no circumstances is the author responsible for any losses, direct or indirect, that are incurred due to the use of the information contained within this document, including, but not limited to, errors, omissions, or inaccuracies.

The trademarks used are without any consent, and the publication of the trademark is without permission or backing by the trademark owner. All trademarks and brands within this book are for clarifying purposes only and are owned by the owners themselves, not affiliated with this document.

Table of Contents

INTRODUCTION 1
BROKEN HEART 3
    Why am I brokenhearted? 5
    How do these two factors break a lover's heart? 10
GETTING PAST YOUR BREAKUP 13
    1) Pick your battles. 14
    2) Don't compare yourself to other people's breakups. ... 14
    3) Don't distract yourself. 15
    4) Let go of everything. 15
    5) Talk to others who've gone through breakups in the past. 15
    6) Don't blame yourself for the breakup. 16
    7) Don't obsess over the situation. 16
    8) Realize that you DIDN'T do anything wrong. 17
5 STAGES OF GRIEVING 19
    Denial 20
    Anger 21
    Bargaining 23
    Depression 24

Acceptance 25

WHY LETTING GO IS HARD 27

You are still mad. 27

You are used to getting everything your way 28

You are left with a lot of unanswered questions. 29

Your ego got crushed 30

HOW TO HEAL FROM HEARTBREAK AND FIND YOUR WAY BACK TO NORMALCY 31

1. You Don't Have To Be Alone: 31

2. Eat A Healthy Dose Of Reality 32

3. Do Something Nice For Someone Else 33

4. Above All Else, Be Honest With Yourself 33

5. Put Your Positive Energy Into A New Relationship ... 34

6. Stay Busy 34

7. Take Time For Yourself 35

8. Focus On Your Goals 35

RELEASE YOURSELF FROM THE GUILT 37

HOW TO DEAL WITH OBSESSING AND FLASHBACKS 45

Intrusion Concept 48

The Meaning of Obsession 49

What Do You Do If You Have Obsessive Thoughts? 50

HOW TO STOP THE PAIN 55

Breathe and place your focus somewhere else. 57

Find a good feeling and chase it...57

The Pleasures of Small Things..58

Make time..58

Volunteer yourself..59

Set a Goal..59

PHASES OF HEALING FROM A BROKEN HEART 61

The Uncovering Phase..64

The Decision Phase 67

The Work Phase...68

MENTAL AND PHYSICAL WORK............................ 73

Mental Work..73

Physical Work..76

The Deepening Phase 82

FORGIVING AND MOVING FORWARD.............. 87

Forgiveness is a Process..89

Is There a Right Time to Forgive?......................................92

FALLING IN LOVE WITH YOURSELF.................... 99

Radical Self-Love...99

The Most Important Relationship.....................................102

Rebuilding Self-Worth..105

Becoming the Person You Love 107

TAKING CARE OF YOURSELF 109

TAKING CARE OF YOUR KIDS 115

What happens to my kids after a breakup? 116

How can I prepare my kids? 116

Don't over-explain or overemphasize the relationship (even though this might feel good). 118

Take care of your health in whatever way is best for you. 119

Learn how to move on when it's time to move on. 120

THE PATH TO FIND TRUE LOVE 121

Acknowledge the pain 123

Stop blaming yourself 124

Think about the future 124

BREAKUP RECOVERY
1 ♥ 1

A tried-and-true strategy for surviving the traumatic end of any romantic relationship, including divorce, along with practical methods for healing, regaining trust, and seeking true love.

It's done, and it hurts a lot. Still, as incredible as it can sound in the midst of heartbreak, you will move on from your breakup. Forget about trying to win back your ex. Forget about losing yourself in the process of trying to make this person love you. Starting today, this breakup is the perfect time to make positive changes in your life, both inside and out.

Nora Williams has helped thousands of people change their love lives through her seminars and counseling activity. Now, in Breakup Recovery 101, she'll show you how to refocus your attention on yourself. Her strategy consists of the following elements:

- Disengagement rules: how and why to go "no-touch" with your ex
- How to work through grief, overcome fear, and reclaim your life
- How to break the cycle of failed relationships
- What to do if you can't stop thinking about your ex, texting, calling, checking their social profile, or driving by their house

INTRODUCTION

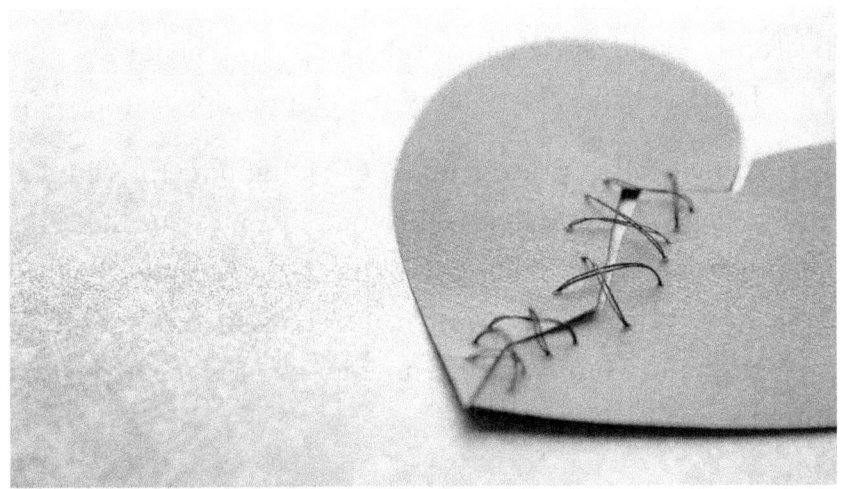

Heartbreak, not one person on this Earth is immune to it. It is an unavoidable part of the human experience. At times, heartbreak can bring real physical pain, like that awful pit in the bottom of your stomach, or those pains in your chest that seemingly come out of nowhere. But what probably hurts the most is the hole your ex leaves behind, the emptiness in your life. The space they used to fill in your day and your life is gone. All you have left are the memories. Without your ex, life seems less enjoyable

Healing from a breakup is difficult, but not impossible. When you've been rejected by someone you love, the pain can feel unbearable, and it may be hard to imagine moving on. But have faith and remember that time is of the essence. The sooner you choose to heal yourself, the better.

In many ways, heartbreak is no different than any other painful life event. It's difficult and life-altering, but it's not permanent or final. There are lots you can do to help yourself heal and rebuild, and there are also steps you can take to give your heart a chance. Here are some helpful tips.

Part of the healing process involves taking time for yourself and letting you think things through. Even if your thoughts keep turning back to them, don't beat yourself up about it! Your heart is incredibly complicated, so sometimes it's hard to separate in your mind the memories of what happened from the reality of who left.

The best thing you can do is force yourself out of this rut, and move on with your life by seeking out healthy relationships instead of dwelling on the past.

Don't let the rest of the world see how truly heartbroken you are over your lost love. It's okay to be sad, but you don't want others to know how much it hurts. Put on a brave face and smile at people approaching you, even if your heart is breaking inside. People will appreciate your upbeat attitude and find it refreshing in comparison to their own sad feelings. Get back to the gym. Exercise is scientifically proven to speed weight loss, help you clear your head and boost your energy levels. Work out three to five times per week for about 30 minutes each time, and you'll see results within a few months that will make you feel better about yourself.

BROKEN HEART

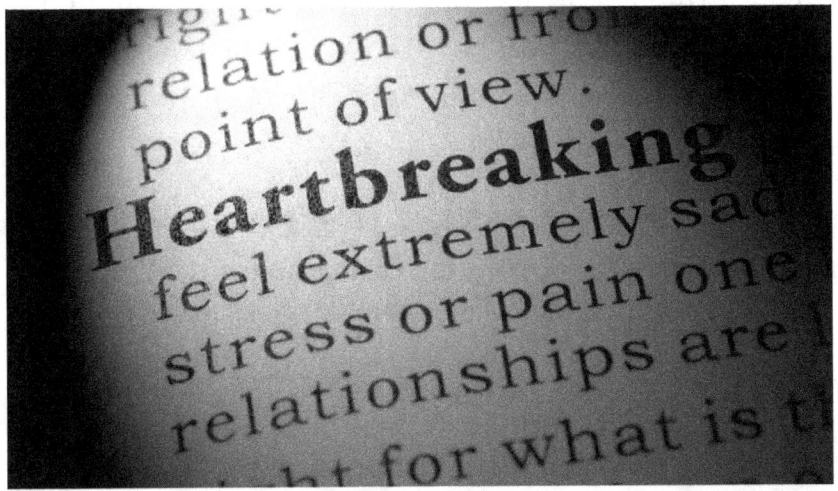

A broken heart, perhaps, is not a phrase we would hear daily, and it is not used in conversation as much as love. It is so because a broken heart tends to be hidden; it is almost a shame to show or express in one or another way. It is like crying; we were taught that crying symbolizes weakness, and a broken heart is a medal for losers. People hide a broken heart like they hide tears.

Some people might say that their hearts were broken while they meant that they were upset, jealous, piqued, or simply sad. They thought their hearts were broken due to the fullness and pain they experienced in their chest or tears rolling down their cheeks. Those are not necessarily the signs of a broken heart. Most of the time, people who said they are heartbroken didn't know that they were not at that level yet.

It is not easy to define and explain what the broken heart is and how it feels like for the experience is somehow beyond any description. The fact that love songs writers and poets use metaphors to describe a broken heart shows that our daily words are not descriptive enough to make it imaginable.

A broken heart is an unexpected experience that can make even the strongest man on the earth find tears rolling down on his face and shake his world. It can make a religious man lose his faith. It can make a professor go dumb. It can make a psychotherapist depressed. And it can make a visionary man commit suicide. If these strong people can be made standing on their knees (or heads), it is not easy to imagine what it can do to common people like us.

At its lowest level, the initial diagnosis of a broken heart is the fullness and pain in the chest. The drastic decrease of appetite and motivation to do what we know or are aware of is essential for our living. It is also a common symptom that a brokenhearted person sleeps more than usual since he wants to escape from a painful reality. The conversation with other people turns less frequent except with someone who knows what is going on and why. Sometimes, having a conversation about what we are experiencing (broken heart) can temporarily release the pain.

Not a few people died due to broken hearts. The doctors and psychologists became alerted to the seriousness of a broken heart to study this experience. Many people were shocked when the result of the study was presented. It has been found that a broken heart is not merely a mental but also a medical condition. It means that the phrase broken heart is no longer a metaphor.

The experts gave broken heart syndrome a name, Takotsubo Cardiomyopathy. It is a weakening of the heart's main pumping chamber due to severe emotional and physical stress. This happens due to the increased cortisol level caused by the limbic system's response to the mental drama of not being loved. The increase in cortisol level leads a heartbroken man to frustration. Since he is frustrated, his immune system drops, and consequently, it does not function optimally. When the human immune system does not function properly, plus the heart's main pumping does not work optimally, we are in a serious medical condition.

Unfortunately, it is an irony that there is no medical treatment to cure a broken heart, although it has been discovered that a broken heart is a medical condition. There is no pill for curing a broken heart. Many men ran to drugs, and those who could not hold it any longer might commit suicide. For many people, a broken heart is the edge of life. Well, I am here to say that it is not.

Why am I brokenhearted?

That your heart is broken is far from my expectation. Therefore, the "I" here means anyone who is experiencing a broken heart. However, the heartbroken people need to read this section and happy persons who believe that despairs of love are out of sight.

In Buddhism, there is no romantic love. Buddhists believe that romantic love is not the true love for this kind of love (Eros) leads us to attachment and compulsion. When we are in love romantically with someone, it is believed, we become compulsive, and for an acceptable reason, we become attached to the person we are in love with. The problem that Buddha pointed is that it is attachment and compulsion that generate suffering. In other words, suffering, including a broken heart, is natural to experience in romantic love. It is so because nothing lasts forever; we will leave (or be left) by the person we love. From this point of view, it is reasonable why a break-up can break the heart. Let's imagine a plaster stick on our skin; when it is detached, we feel pain.

Based on the principle above, Buddha taught unconditional love or love without expecting any return. Of course, Buddha was not the only one. Jesus, Rumi, and Muhammad (PBUH) also taught the same love. However, not all people are sages and mystics; we are only common people experiencing love as human beings. Although our hearts do not need any return, our bodies have a different call. For example, though felt in the heart, longing is a call to the bodily presence of someone we are longing for. Our bodies call for touches, hugs, or kisses from the one we have Eros on. If these calls are unanswered, the soul (spiritual love) and the body (romantic love) will go through different paths. Unfortunately, as long as we are in the body, it is somehow irrational to feel nothing but causeless bliss without hard work. Therefore, loving unconditionally, for some people, can be the worst episode in their life.

Therefore, a broken heart is a possible risk in romantic love; it is even more possible than happiness. I always reconsider my thought when asked if romantic love is not true love for love is divided into different types and forms, as discussed above. The only fake love in my mind is when you love someone, but only you take advantage of the relationship.

Two main factors cause your heart to be broken. The first cause is any hurtful action done by the one you love, and the second cause is a separation (break up, divorce, cheated, death, etc.). However, these two causes are given power by expectation and attachment.

Eros is a physical and mental call that unconsciously needs to be answered. Naturally, our bodies are longing for hugs and kisses because they are designed that way. In having Eros, a strong one, it is very ordinary to have some expectations like being answered, accepted, touched, hugged, kissed and loved (by the one who the Eros is destined to). Our minds give these bodily needs meaning as valuable and sacred things to experience. According to the Law of Emotion, as explained by psychologist Nico Frijda, our emotion toward something or someone or an experience is determined by the meaning we give to it. When we change the meaning of something or someone, our emotions toward them will change accordingly. Expectation is a meaning given by our minds to anything that we expect to happen or experience. If the expectation is not achieved, then the opposite emotion emerges. For example, let's say that you expect a hug from the one you love. In your mind, a hug from her will put you blissful. When she rejects to hug you, the opposite emotion emerges (e.g., sorrow).

The deeper the meaning you give to your lover's hug, the stronger your emotion will be. The stronger your emotion against your lover's hug, the stronger your expectations will be. The stronger your expectations for your lover's hug, the more you are at risk for heartbreak if your expectations are not fulfilled.

When we fall in love with someone, we never count our expectations in our minds and hearts. What we consciously have in our mind is a dream if the love is answered. Unconsciously, the expectations are pictured in the dream. We may have hundreds of expectations if we try to unmerge the pictures in our dream of love. Each expectation plays its role in building the dream we wish to come true. Each expectation, eventually, is potentially the cause of both our happiness and sorrows.

One of the natures of expectation is that it is limitless; it grows. When an expectation is fulfilled, another expectation grows. I had seen (and experienced by myself) that many lovers were broken far before their love answered. This is due to the first factor, unfulfilled expectation. Nevertheless, just because your Eros is answered, it does not mean that your expectation is fulfilled forever. You may expect other things like loyalty, availability, and so on. You will start to compel your partner to be available or present anytime you need her, be loyal, be sexy, and so on. You may put different expectations on different levels. When the higher expectation like loyalty is not fulfilled one day, then you fall into sorrow again.

Your lover may always fulfill your expectations until one day you find yourself attached to that person. You become so dependent on that person until you find yourself in pieces, and only that person can make you feel like a whole. When it comes, you are already in the higher stage and are introduced to the second factor of heartbreak, attachment.

What makes attachment a factor of heartbreak is separation. When you are strongly attached to your lover, you have given her your power button. You will be like a damaged battery notebook that always needs to be plugged into the electricity terminal to switch on. Your consumptive behavior causes this; it happens because you disobey the sacred rule of love that it always gives, and it never asks. Even if you are in Eros, you need to cultivate love within yourself to take and give love equally. If you are always in the taking or receiving position, separation will certainly "kill" you. In the end, separation is also a specific experience.

How do these two factors break a lover's heart?

Heartbreak commonly occurs gradually, although certain dramatic, sorrowful experiences can cause it spontaneously. The mild knocks to the heart "wall" mentally create minor rifts like jealousy or mild sadness. If you choose to forgive or forget the event, the rifts will likely be healed in no time. However, if the events endure and you take them seriously, then the rifts will develop. Your imagination may play an important role in deepening the emotional impact of the events, which in turn widens the rifts or add new rifts. For example, due to the "secret" chats you found on your spouse's inbox, in the next day, you perhaps imagine if your spouse is going with someone else to the movie while it is not necessarily true; this will surely worsen the rifts.

Gradual heartbreak occurs through small events that threaten your expectation and pull you away from your partner. However, it is your mind that worsens your emotion. You can see that forgiving and forgetting are two mind works; they ease your emotion. However, if your mind works against yourself (e.g., making you miserable by showing you your spouse's mistakes), you will worsen your emotional condition. Moreover, it will endure your heart pain and make you roll into the torturing emotional turmoil. When you constantly experience the emotional turmoil in your heart, you will experience higher-level pain like resentment and even depression.

Time, sometimes, does not heal the wound in the heart. Active participation in putting bandages on the wounds is needed. Forgiveness and letting go are recommended mainly by psychologists and spiritualists around the world, as we will go through in the other section.

Due to the resentment or depression you experience that you don't take care of, you will likely experience heartbreak, which is described as Takotsubo Cardiomyopathy. In other words, you will transfer your experience from mental heartbreak to medical heartbreak.

Certain dramatic events can cause heartbreak in the first knock. What are the dramatic events in question? It may be vulgar to put the examples, so I let you fill in the blanks. However, there is no universal list of dramatic events that cause spontaneous heartbreak; there is no exact definition because different people define it differently. I define it as the most unexpected events threatening your expectations and pulling you away from your partner. Based on that definition, the more it threatens your expectations, the more dramatic the event.

A small event like coming late can be interpreted as a dramatic event to some people who interpret the late coming as spending the time with another person and leaving just "leftover" for them. Since different people may interpret events differently, the most available definition of dramatic event, which can cause heartbreak in the first knock, is the most unexpected event that threatens the expectation and attachment the most. It is theatrical and intense.

If you are observant enough, you will see that the main factors of heartbreak are expectation and attachment. However, what makes it worse and deeper is your mind. It was said that your mind is both your best friend and worst enemy.

GETTING PAST YOUR BREAKUP

The pain of a breakup can be rough. It feels like the world is crashing down, and there's nothing you can do to stop it, but this isn't true in many ways. Yes, it's tough to move forward from falling out of love and being left behind by someone you were once so close with. But it's also necessary.

Breakups are altogether different for everyone; there are no one-size-fits-all solutions for overcoming them, and everyone handles them differently. Some people may be able to speak with friends about the matter, while others might not want anyone in their life other than their cat (or dog) until they've healed enough.

In any case, if you're ready to move past this breakup, here are some things that may help get you through the next few weeks.

1) Pick your battles.

Whether it's a text back or how your friends respond to breaking up with you, there will be moments in time where you will feel compelled to reach out and talk to your ex. These instances are the ones where it's best not to overreact and let things resolve themselves naturally. You don't want either one of you making a quick snap decision that will end up making the situation worse for both parties involved. When you're trying to heal from a breakup, don't let yourself be pushed into overreacting because of fear or guilt...trust that both of you are moving in the right direction.

2) Don't compare yourself to other people's breakups.

Only YOU are going through this, so it's essential to not spend too much time thinking about what other people are doing or struggling with. Sure, there may be some similarities between your situation and somebody else, but you have to be strong enough to know there is no room for comparison. No two breakups are identical; only you can determine how yours ended up and what worked best for you in the long run. You don't need anybody else reminding you how you should feel or what would have been a better outcome if only things had turned out differently.

3) Don't distract yourself.

This breakup is still fresh, and there are a lot of emotions being felt by the two people involved, so you must remain focused on working through this challenging time as gracefully as possible. You don't need to beat yourself up for what you did or didn't do to help the situation, but don't allow yourself to overdo it either. There are no deadlines for when this breakup has to be resolved, so let yourself take some time out to heal from the trauma and make sure that your body is ready for another round.

4) Let go of everything.

This is easier said than done, but you'll be glad when you take this step because it will allow you to keep your mind off the situation. You want to feel like the breakup has already happened and think about it as little as possible. There will be a lot of time for you to think about what happened later, so for now, focus on putting your physical and emotional energy into something that can make you feel better.

5) Talk to others who've gone through breakups in the past.

The advice from those people who have been there before can be invaluable in helping you deal with this challenging time ... while at least not making things worse by talking too much about it with whoever is listening (which is always a good rule). If you have some friends who have gone through breakups, there's a good chance that they will be more than willing to offer some advice on how you can overcome your own personal struggles. Even if you don't reach out to anyone, in particular, it's a good idea to just spend time with others and keep your mind occupied so that you don't try to spend too much time dwelling on the past.

6) Don't blame yourself for the breakup.

You need to let go of the belief that THERE IS ONLY ONE PERSON AT FAULT for this breakup happening...it just doesn't work like that. You are responsible for putting yourself in this situation, so you need to move forward with that in mind. You can't feel like you're stuck in a corner because of something that happened last week or last year ... you're not a victim, and it's your responsibility to deal with this.

7) Don't obsess over the situation.

You want to be able to move past the breakup as quickly as possible and start focusing on other things, so don't allow yourself to be consumed by thoughts of how the two of you used to be together or what would have happened if things were different. There's no use dwelling on this ... just move forward.

8) Realize that you DIDN'T do anything wrong.

This breakup is on you, so there's no need for you to feel guilty for what happened or any mistakes you may have made along the way. You know that this relationship had a particular outcome and ending, and it's not something anyone can control. So don't let it get to you. You will be fine on your own and deserve to start creating new plans for your life without having to worry about filling the void left behind by the end of the relationship.

FIVE STAGES OF GRIEVING

Grieving is a normal part of life, and it is customary to grieve or mourn if we lose somebody or experience something sad or painful.

With that said, it is crucial that while you are living through the aftermath of your breakup, we don't want to skip over the grieving process. You need to grieve, or all those feelings will sneak up on you when you are least prepared for them. You need to deal with it now.

Some people think that recovering from a breakup is as easy as a snap of a finger. They believe that when they take you to a bar to drink and meet some eligible bachelor that you will be just peachy the next day. Unfortunately, that isn't the case. In fact, it is better if you stick with the process of grief and not skip over it all in favor of ignoring it ever happened.

Instead, put a rain check on your friends' bar hopping escapades for now. Take time to recover from the breakup.

Here are the five steps of grief that everyone going through the same situation as you will follow. You can take time with each step and make sure you understand that there is no hurrying to this process. There is no predetermined amount of time to grieve.

Denial

This is the part where the initial shock of the breakup plays its part. The minute you hear your guy leaving or breaking up with you, you will not immediately believe it. It will simply not sink in.

Give your mind the chance to catch up with what happened. Take a few deep breaths and process the words and actions while giving your brain the chance to let it sink in. Denial is essentially a safety net. It gives you the chance to work through the situation without feeling too deeply until you are ready to process the emotions. Don't diminish your relationship or pretend it never happened as part of the denial phase. Don't try and continue the numbness denial brings by imbibing too much or using drugs. Let it run its course.

Anger

You can say that you are on this stage when you are mad at your ex for making you go through what you are going through right now. In the previous stage, you were not feeling angry because you were still taking it all in. You weren't feeling much of anything in that initial phase. Now that all the denial has faded, you are mad as heck!

Don't worry about it. It is ok to feel angry, and it is a natural process that you have to get through. Control your anger and do not do anything that will make your grief worse, like doing something illegal. Always keep your anger in check.

The best and quickest way to get beyond this stage is to release that anger constructively.

The important thing you are going to want to do is either open up a blank document on your laptop or grab a pencil and paper.

Begin by addressing the letter to your ex. Why are you writing a letter? It's hard to be honest with others and even harder to be honest with ourselves. However, a private letter gives us a safe place to let out our emotions and express the things that we never had a chance or the courage to say.

Start the letter by letting out all the thoughts and emotions that are currently inside of you. Write out your frustrations, write out your fears about the relationship, write out why you are upset.

Do you want to scream at him? Write it out.

Are you confused? Write it out.

Does he make you feel like crying when you think about him? Write it out.

Again, be very honest with yourself here because, to heal, you have to remove the bad things to clean the wound.

Next, in the same letter, write down everything that you learned as a result of your relationship with him. Not just the things you learned to avoid but also the things you learned about *yourself*. List out as many lessons that come to mind.

Finally, end the letter by thanking him for the lessons that the relationship enabled you to learn. In your own words, tell him that you forgive him for any hurt that he has caused you. Wish him the best and acknowledge to him that you are letting him go and moving forward with your life.

Once the letter is complete, read it aloud to yourself.

Read it with all the emotions residing within you and feel each one being released with each word. You might find it difficult to get through the letter, and that's okay. Keep reading it until you can read the letter in a clear, strong voice. As you read it through the final time, acknowledge the words and their meaning. Let it resound not only in your ears but also in your heart.

After reading the letter, delete it. Or if you wrote it, rip up the letter and throw it away.

This is very important because you let go and release the hold that your unexpressed emotions had on you.

Then, take a deep breath and relax. Releasing emotions is never an easy task, so be sure to reward yourself for taking such a big step to healing.

Other Ideas to Release Negative Energy

Go for a hike, get on the treadmill or scrub your kitchen from top to bottom. Release all that energy you have your anger fuels that. It also helps to talk it out with a good friend. Acknowledge the anger, release it and move forward into your new life.

Bargaining

Now that you are no longer angry, you are probably thinking, "Hey, wait, I want you and I will do whatever it takes to be with you." You long for those moments in the relationship when everything seemed so great and are ready to bargain with him to get those moments back.

Your willingness to sacrifice and change just to get him back is now obvious. You might even come to a point when you are willing to forget all that he has done in order to get him back. You must hold on, I know I told you that this is a stage that you have to encounter, but this doesn't mean that you can get on your knees and beg him to love you again. It does not work that way. You can certainly change those things about you that maybe he said he didn't like, but do it for you — not him.

The changes you were willing to make for him can be used as a tool to help you through this stage of grief. Maybe you promised to get in better shape. That is an excellent goal but ensure you are doing it so *you* feel better. Join a gym and go for it. Consider taking up a hobby that will make you feel more fulfilled. It is all about you and your own health and wellbeing. Make a bargain with *yourself* to feel better.

Depression

Now comes the sad part. What will you be left with when all the anger fades away and all your bargaining ideas are shunned? I know you answered, "Nothing." While that isn't the least bit true, you won't immediately believe it and will inevitably begin the depression phase.

Don't force yourself to go out and mingle with other people just to "look ok" when you are crumbling inside. Whoever said that locking yourself up in your room is a bad idea doesn't know what he is talking about. Go ahead, isolate yourself from people and spend some time alone. It is ok to cry. Just don't spend years inside your room, and make sure you take care of yourself through the process.

Although this is probably the most miserable stage of grief, it is a part of the healing process. The best thing you can do is acknowledge the loss and the feelings associated with it and keep moving forward. Do your best to maintain normal routines, and eventually, you will heal and move on to the final stage of grief.

Acceptance

This is what you are aiming for. When you have finally realized that you are only hurting yourself while you are skulking in your room while your ex is out there enjoying his life and being seen in every bar and dancing with every woman he meets, then it is time to get out and enjoy your single life.

It is necessary that during this time, you focus solely on improving yourself and not your ex. Why? Because when he gets tired of his nightly party and he spends his nights alone in his room, that's when he will realize what he lost. You chose to take your time getting through the process and coming out on the other side as a healthy person once again. He, however, is going to be bombarded with those feelings because he ignored them. So when he calls and asks you to reconcile, you won't be there. You will be somewhere, enjoying your single life and not caring about him.

Acceptance doesn't mean you like what happened, but you have realized it is what it is. Your life is going on just fine without him. You are not thinking about him or what he did every moment of the day. Maintaining routines and enjoying life is the best way to reach acceptance. Live your life for *yourself* and fall in love with the new, stronger woman whom you have become.

WHY LETTING GO IS HARD

Now that you understand the importance of shifting your mindset and are ready to take the next step into the journey of letting go, you need to address a couple of other things. You have to determine why you are having a hard time letting go. I'll give you four common reasons why it can be hard to let go an ex. Assess what you are feeling and pinpoint the most probable one. Once you know the reason why, you can take action to move past it.

You are still mad.

Anger is a really heavy anchor that might be preventing you from moving on. If you spend every day feeling angry and focusing on how you feel about what he said or did, then you might just be sinking yourself deeper into the muck of an ended relationship.

In order to move beyond your anger, you have to accept and forgive. Accept that what happened is in the past, and focus your mind on *your* future. There is absolutely nothing you can do to change it, and it does not deserve your time, energy or happiness. The pain will not go away unless you forgive and let go of your anger. We will explore how to let go of this anger in a later chapter.

You are used to getting everything your way.

You can't believe he left you. You can't believe he broke up with you and broke your heart. You can't believe how he had the nerve to do it. To *you*, of all people!

Admittedly, people who are used to getting exactly what they want are going to struggle a bit. Those who never knew defeat usually find it hard to move on, especially when they were the ones left by their ex. If you are one of these people, I want you to remember how you learned to walk. You fell down, remember? No matter how much it hurt, you got back up and kept moving.

Our adult life is no different; we will fall down at some point, but in picking ourselves up, we become stronger. Like a tiny step forward, you recognize what works for you and what doesn't.

Being in denial and blind to that fact to this crucial learning curve anchors you to your pain and prevents you from letting go. Accept this as a fact of life, and when you do, you will be able to let go.

You are left with a lot of unanswered questions.

Do you feel that your break-up was so sudden that it just came out of nowhere? Were you lost when he broke up with you? Maybe you felt as if you got hit by a runaway train you never saw coming. Did the anger and hurt get the better of you, and you stormed off and left him or vice versa?

Relationships ending in this way are usually the ones that leave a lot of unanswered questions. Instead of talking about the problem, the couple was consumed by pain and anger that they both walked away from the "talk."

Often, if this is the case, you will be too stuck with the questions you have to be able to fully let go.

If you can, try to have a "serious talk" with your ex, not to reconcile, but to answer some questions. If that is not possible, try answering the questions yourself. Contemplate your past relationship and see if you can answer your questions. Just make sure that you don't blame yourself for everything. Once you have a good idea about why the relationship didn't last, you will be ready to head down the path of letting go.

Your ego got crushed

You may not want to admit it, but you have an ego. We all do. Sometimes our egos can be our own worst enemies. A big ego often results in somebody trying to manipulate another person or do things they normally wouldn't because their ego got a little bruised.

When a person has a big ego and is thrust into a situation where they are humiliated or hurt, it stings. A common response is to lash out at the person who damaged the ego. The pain from the blow to the ego makes it difficult to move on and let go of the relationship.

If you feel that you are this kind of person, you have to let go of your ego first before letting go of the whole relationship. As long as you stay mad because of your crushed ego, you will not be able to move on.

Try to think of it like this; it isn't personal. It did not happen to you because you did something or didn't do something. It is just how things are, sometimes you win, and sometimes you don't get your way. Accept it and acknowledge that your ego took a little beating, but you will not let it hold you down.

Once you have determined the reason why you can't let go of your recent break-up, you can concentrate on moving on.

HOW TO FIND YOUR WAY BACK TO NORMALCY

Healing from a breakup can be difficult, but it is not impossible. When you've been rejected by someone you love, the pain can feel unbearable, and it may be hard to imagine moving on. But have faith! Please read on as we discuss how to heal from a heartbreak and find your way back to normalcy.

1. You Don't Have To Be Alone:

You can make it through the first few days after being dumped with ease with a little preparation.

It can be difficult to accept that the person you love with all your heart has moved on when you are heartbroken, and this is because emotions and logic tend to fight for control. When you are filled thinking negative thoughts such as "I can't believe they did that to me," or "I don't deserve this," try not to listen to them. They are simply your mind's way of trying to convince you that what's happened is your fault or that it wasn't meant to happen at all.

These are little ways our minds try to convince us of these limiting thoughts, but we have no reason to believe them. Of course, it's okay to feel sad about being dumped, but try not to let yourself get lost in the sadness. Instead of dwelling on the pain, take a step back and start believing that you deserve better. This is a reminder that other people in the world are capable of loving and caring for you. We need the last option to feel bad about ourselves when so many good people are out there.

2. Eat A Healthy Dose Of Reality

When you've been rejected, it's probably safe to assume that your ex has moved on too.

In this type of situation, it's best not to protest or try to win them back. Trying to convince them that you are right for them will only cause more pain and sadness. It's never easy to face the truth, but the sooner you accept that they aren't coming back, the better off you'll be.

3. Do Something Nice For Someone Else

Give yourself a little bit of time to heal from your breakup before starting a new relationship.

When we're in a relationship with someone we love, we often forget how great it is to help and care for others. We tend to think about ourselves instead of all of the wonderful things that go along with being selfless and compassionate.

Try volunteering at a local shelter or charity organization instead of sitting around feeling heartbroken (which you are allowed to do). You don't have to wait until you are dating again. a lot of people are out there who could use your help and support. When you focus on other people's needs of others, it's amazing what can happen.

4. Above All Else, Be Honest With Yourself

Don't over-think the situation or what went wrong with your relationship.

When you're trying to move on from your ex, it can be easy to think about all of the things they did that hurt you or made you unhappy with them. When you're analyzing the relationship, try to see the situation from a new perspective. Try to avoid "what if" thinking because it is not productive and can make you feel worse.

The main thing we want to avoid when we're heartbroken is becoming bitter. The best way to recover from heartbreak is to remember that the next time around will be better than the last. Being bitter only makes things worse in every aspect of your life.

5. Put Your Positive Energy Into A New Relationship

Remember, you deserve to be happy! Putting your energy into a new relationship will help you forget about the last one.

A new relationship is the best way to replace negative thoughts with positive ones. When we're in love, there is nothing but positives in our lives. Unfortunately, it's easy to forget this when we've been rejected and find ourselves wallowing in self-pity instead of enjoying life the way we should be.

6. Stay Busy

When it comes to getting over a broken heart, staying busy is important! Don't let yourself sit around and feel sorry for yourself all day long because it will only prolong your sadness.

Sometimes, it's easier to keep our minds occupied with busy work than it is to sit around full of regret and sadness. As much as we might like to, there is no way around the pain of a breakup. The sooner we accept that nothing will change what happened or make us feel any better, the sooner we can pass through this phase in our lives and move on.

7. Take Time For Yourself

We live in a world where it's easy to get caught up in other people's problems all day long, but sometimes, you can easily become overwhelmed if you don't put your needs first. Everyone needs their space, even when they are hundreds of miles apart from one another.

Remember, breaking up with someone doesn't mean that you have to quit having fun. You don't have to put your life on hold for the next few weeks or months until you get over the break-up. Taking it easy or being selfish won't make you feel better; it will only make the pain more intense when you inevitably go back out into the dating world.

8. Focus On Your Goals

When we're heartbroken, it's also very easy to forget what's important in life and start focusing on our feelings more than anything else. However, when you're in a relationship that you put more emphasis on than your own goals and dreams, it's easy to forget that. Taking some days to think about your motivations for staying in a relationship will be very beneficial for finding clarity on where you're going in life and who you want to start dating.

RELEASE YOURSELF FROM THE GUILT

Guilt is a useless emotion, and forgiveness is the cornerstone of healing. So forgive yourself. We are all human, and many times in this life, we will fall short of perfection. I know I have had my moments of being a little too clingy, a little too jealous, and other moments that were not exactly shining. But, I have also been kind and loving and patient when my partner wasn't their best either. It is easy to revisit and mentally rehash those moments and try and find ways that you are unlovable and unworthy, but I assure you, you are not. Set yourself free from those past regrets. That feeling that things could have turned out differently if only you had been better or behaved a certain way. . We end up regretting our decisions because we believe we should have made different ones. We think we should have done something different, but we didn't, or that we should have done something better, but we didn't. We regret some of these decisions, which are in the past and cannot be reversed because we are comparing them to a hypothetical ideal course that we believe we should have followed.

If you find yourself repeating negative patterns, it's time to examine yourself and determine why you're acting this way. The majority of bad conduct and poor decisions stem from a fear of some kind (refer back to the emotion and feeling wheel). What exactly are you afraid of? Whenever we are trying to defend ourselves from anything, we can act out. Our brain attempts to shield us from things that we believe or suspect could harm us.

There's no reason to feel remorseful or guilty. This relationship was and always will be a part of your growth, and you will benefit from it. It does not seem so now, but it will.

So release it.

Breakups, unfortunately, are like death, a mourning of a life you have only glimpsed. The future you envisioned with that person, the memories you planned to have all died, and it can come suddenly and without warning to one of you. Once the shock is gone, you have to release it. I know it hurts, but lean into it and allow yourself to feel it. Trust me, if anyone on this Earth has been lucky enough to experience love, then they have also likely experienced similar heartbreak. It will be okay, you will be okay, you will survive this, and you will thrive again.

Make peace with what was, however beautiful, and know that it will never be again with that person.

Sticks and stones

We have heard this old adage, "Sticks and stones may break my bones, but words can never hurt me." Well, unfortunately, that saying isn't entirely accurate. Words hurt. They can cut deeply and leave scars that last a lifetime. During your breakup, the other person may never say an unkind word about you. They may tell you something like, "It's not you; it's me." In this scenario, your ex likely didn't want to insult you or hurt your feelings. I once had a man tell me one of the reasons he didn't want to be with me was because I had accomplished nothing in the time that he had known me. Ouch! Here I was, a mother raising two lovely children, a homeowner with a great career who has lived a pretty awesome life full of travel and awesome adventures, and this person I respected so much pretty much reduced me to nothing. It hurt, and I have to admit it threw me for a loop. Was it true? Was I this lazy person who had done nothing with their life? Looking back on it, I see how ridiculous it was to let those words bother me so much, but that is the thing with words. They have power, and they can hurt. Harsh words can be confusing, especially if they are coming from someone we love.

Try to remember that this person you love so much is also a flawed human being, prone to say or do anything in the midst of a breakup. Things can get ugly, or heated and they may say hurtful things that you had no idea they were feeling. Do your best to give those words little power over your life. Remember that your ex was likely hurting or angry in some way as well and could be looking to make you feel bad.

It helped me tremendously to categorize the things that were said to me. I asked myself these questions:

Was it honest? Honest words can be held up as a holy grail, and it is a truth that cannot be denied. There are factual truths in life, like when someone arrived somewhere or what you ate for dinner. There is also feedback, and feedback tends to be more of a perspective, which is each person's way of seeing things. So sometimes, "being honest" is just giving an opinion.

For example, "you've accomplished nothing" is actually a perspective. From my ex's viewpoint, he was always taught to strive for a lucrative career and numerous accolades. But I was raised in a large family where everyone gets married, has children, and buys a comfortable home. Having a comfortable home and family to return to at the end of the day is indeed a major accomplishment.

Was it constructive criticism? Constructive criticism is a little different and can be more useful than just criticism. Constructive criticism is when someone considers and fully understands all sides of a situation before offering their opinion. They consider the positives and negatives and make it clear they are only offering their take on things as they offer their viewpoints. Knowing that someone has considered all sides allows you to see ways forward and to feel supported.

Criticism can be useful if given fairly; oftentimes, we tend to forget this and receive everything negatively during a breakup. Even constructive criticism can feel hurtful when this happens, even though the other person sees themselves as trying to help us.

Was it verbal abuse? With verbal abuse, the abuser intends to, whether they realize it or not, hurt and possibly control the person they offer their 'feedback' to. Verbal abuse, also sometimes called emotional abuse, also tends to criticize you as a person, not just what you did and the consequences of the action. And like all forms of abuse, verbal abuse is a way to take power over another by belittling or hurting them.

Some experts think verbal/Emotional abuse to be worse than physical abuse because physical wounds can heal. In contrast, emotional abuse can have long-term effects on the victim, some lasting a lifetime. If you find yourself questioning your perceptions, abilities, intuition, or gut feelings, or have low or no self-esteem. This may be an indicator of some sort of emotional abuse.

Don't allow anyone to tear you down with their words. Remember, you are worthy of so much. You deserve happiness and positivity in a healthy relationship. You deserve to be treated with respect. You deserve it all.

Speak Kindness over yourself

Treat yourself like someone you love. Practice being your own best friend. How would you talk to a friend struggling through a breakup? No matter the circumstances of your breakup, now is the time to reassure yourself that you are worth being cared for. Love is still available to you. You are still enough, despite what may have been said or done to you. The inner

deep dialogue you have with yourself is critical right now. Be kind and tolerant with yourself.

Challenge yourself to speak kindly to yourself during this time. You must let go of any negative messages from your ex. The more you dwell on and repeat any negative messages, the more your brain finds evidence to support them, and the more it begins to believe them, even if they were never true in the first place. Many of us have been conditioned to apologize and beat ourselves up when someone speaks poorly of us, but it's possible to change that behavior. Speak kindness over your life! When you speak kindly to yourself on a consistent basis, you can experience higher levels of self-worth, more confidence, happiness, and less stress. Remember, there isn't a relationship in the world that is more important than the one you have with yourself.

Below are some examples of kind things you can say about yourself:

- The world needs my light.
- I am unique.
- I can, and I will do something to promote healing in my life.
- I can handle anything - one step at a time.
- I deserve to be loved.
- I am enough.
- I get better every single day.
- I love who I am.
- I am proud of myself.
- I am all the light I need.

DEAL WITH OBSESSING AND FLASHBACKS

Post-traumatic reactions can last days, weeks, months, or even years. Even though no two traumas are alike, the symptoms of trauma are remarkably consistent. Couples who are healing from a lover's deception must hear and appreciate the tale in its most detailed explanations. Your explanation of your surroundings and your use of eyes and ears to keep track of your partner's actions stems from a fair fear of being betrayed again. Flashbacks are triggered by even the tiniest uncertainty or signs of worsening in the situation. Coping strategies necessitate a balance between the confirmation, regulation, and management of these reactions. As a result of betrayal and being manipulated by those you loved and trusted the most. Lily, a therapist friend of mine, came to me and told me she had been through two traumatic experiences in a short period of time. When she opened her car door and turned the key in the ignition, a man sitting in the passenger seat with a short gun told her to be completely silent and pointed a gun at her head. She was frightened. Lily gasped as the light turned red in central Washington, DC, and he jumped down, then grabbed her purse as the light green was about to turn green.

As terrifying as this had been for Lily, she said that because of her profession, she was able to recover more quickly from this incident than from her partner's ignorant betrayal of her trust, whom she loved and trusted. Intimate relationship betrayal has long-term consequences. When a pistol was pointed directly at her head, Lily believed she could protect herself from the repercussions of the horrific incident she had experienced. She was less secure in her ability to protect herself because her car door was closed, but she persevered. On the other hand, coping with memories with information about her partner's cheating was even more complicated for her. She was frustrated with how little control she appeared to have over her feelings and how long it took her to recover. It's important to realize that feeling disoriented and confused is completely normal. You and your partner are most likely not insane, and your irrational feelings will pass. One of the ironies of recovery from a partner's deception is that the involved/betraying partner will emerge as the hero, becoming more compassionate and empathetic. This suggests that betrayed partners are vulnerable due to the root of danger; they are more likely to become obsessed and have memories of their loss. On the other hand, engaging in these obsessive thoughts can be challenging for the individual concerned. As a result, they devote all of their efforts to make amends with their betrayed spouse.

After the betrayal is revealed, the betraying partner may undergo distressing mental, physical, and emotional changes for the first year. You can believe you're fine: the affair is over, so you can speak more freely. But you're still afraid that these feelings will return and that you'll have to go through all the agony again? These traumatic reactions are common, but they will fade with time. First, the frequency of flashbacks and obsessive thoughts decreases; second, the length of flashbacks and obsessive thoughts decreases.

Last but not least, you must reduce the severity of your symptoms, after which you can begin to see signs of recovery. Interference, restraint, and hyperarousal are three forms of post-traumatic reactions. If the danger is physical or life-threatening, these responses are medically classified as post-traumatic stress disorder (PTSD). On the other hand, these tragedies often show the same clusters of symptoms, which can last for longer periods.

Intrusion Concept

Intrusion is exacerbated by traumatic images associated with deceit, such as the time of discovery, perceived intimacy in a situation, or the string of lies leading up to the revelation. You experience the psychological pain of a traumatic incident as you recall your dream and hallucinations. Television conference shows, love songs, and even ordinary physical objects that were innocent before the revelation appear to be charged with deception. Love scenes in films can conjure up vivid images of illicit sex. In a patriotic voice, the word "loyalty" can elicit a flurry of unwanted thoughts about the relationship and trends involved. Since details are simplified and re-examined, the tape of betrayal continues to play, almost indefinitely, a never-ending series of events in mind. Belinda found it tough to work through her husband's one-year love affair. An intercepted love note had piqued her interest. Even though he said he was not emotionally involved with the other woman, his passionate and loving language told a different story. She was haunted by her husband's poetry, which she had never heard for herself. Belinda endured even more agony, believing he was intimate with his affair partner but not with her. Every time she talked to her husband, his assurances seemed empty and hollow. Belinda kept the love letter in her possession for a long time.

The Meaning of Obsession

Partners who have been betrayed cannot avoid obsessing about the affair until they have all the answers, which may take months. They are always inquiring about lies and unanswered questions. Visual images, dialog snippets, and perplexing memories fixate and obsess them. They leave a significant amount of time to uncovering the truth about previous deceptions. To reconstruct the events that occurred, they question and examine all of the events in their lives that were previously completely significant. It's fairly typical for women to become obsessive during periods of emotional stress while men suppress their emotions. It's the difference between the individual who says, "I'll come across the bridge," and the person who asks, "What is the way to the bridge? What is the layout of the bridge? What color is it?" Ruminators examine, re-examine, and assess disturbing incidents, while suppressors focus on preventing them. Regardless of gender, the betraying partner suppresses the affair, while the betrayed partner obsesses over it.

To escape responsibility, the betraying partner can promote forgetting by denying or downplaying the treason's severity. Before disclosing their relationship, betrayed spouses do everything possible to prevent or ignore their betrayed partner's worries or doubts. Standard apologies are made, claiming that the affair was minor or insignificant; the betrayed partner blames the betraying partner; the betrayed partner insists on taking more time to reconcile and then move on. They try to keep their shame a secret — anything to avoid having the same chapter and verse read over and over again.

What Do You Do If You Have Obsessive Thoughts?

It's important to realize that pathologically obsessive thinking may not result in trauma, and it's a well-known reality. Before taking steps to deal with broken hopes and create a story about the affair, people are prone to anxiety. This means that obsessive thoughts will obstruct the entire rehabilitation process until it is completed. However, they appear to subside in a marriage as long as harmony and transparency are preserved. When disruptive ideas become too noisy or intrusive, it is essential to control optimistic and productive thoughts. Others have learned from a few of the strategies mentioned below.

Retrospectives

Obsessive impulses can be regulated to some extent. Flashes, on the other hand, are sporadic, vivid images in which traumatic situations recur. These flashbacks can be triggered by sight, sound, scent, or physical sensations. Nellie, a young lady, climbed onto a porch where her best friend, Ina, had been assassinated by a jealous partner. Years later, Nellie couldn't figure out why any apprehension at the assassination scene immediately took her back to her friend's memories. She had no idea how it was connected to her trauma. Finally, Nellie recalled under hypnosis that the person who killed Ina had pulled her off the porch and into the surrounding woods by grabbing her wrist. Flashbacks can be triggered by some hint of infidelity, regardless of how transparent the evidence is. Flashbacks are upsetting because they occur suddenly and without notice. For a traumatized individual, life is a minefield of explosive causes. And it might be anything: the smell of burning leaves, a busy mobile phone signal, or a thank you dinner message.

Flashbacks and tremors can be triggered by a restaurant you both used to enjoy. It doesn't matter if you have a flashback; what matters now is that you know the truth and that things have begun to turn around. Anna awoke at midnight one night to discover that her husband had not yet gone to bed. When she awoke, she discovered that the light in his computer room was turned on, but the door was shut. She was attempting to use the key. Despite the fact that she was certain her husband had ended his affair and was likely working on a computer project, the locked door made her nervous. It reminded him of the times when he used to lock himself up at 3 a.m. Indulge in his affair, online, in his research. The physical effects that followed the initial trauma came to Anna that night, unlike other memories. She was terrified, panicked, and angry, even though she knew his affair was over.

Constriction

Signs of constriction are inhibition of thoughts, sensations, and activities related to the traumatic event. Many traumatized people describe their feeling of numbness, display little consideration for regular tasks in life, and get separated from others. Most people who have been betrayed switch between repetitive thoughts and feelings on the one hand and constrictive symptoms of avoidance and withdrawal on the other hand. While constriction is most common during the early period, while you suspect something is wrong, it may undoubtedly happen after unfaithfulness has been revealed, with signs that something is wrong but is being ignored. Tiredness caused by anxiety about trauma or betrayal can lead to a state in which one does not want to think, hear, or speak. After all, the high drama sounds like a mental constraint: to feel nothing, inability to think. Typically, this is a temporary state. The betrayed partner seems unexplainably quiet, expresses no feelings, asks no questions, shows almost no emotions after the affair is disclosed.

It can be a safeguard against events too intense or painful to bear, but recovery from infidelity depends mostly on the involved partner in the affair as they are the source of trauma. The emotionally restricted partner gradually thaws and gets angry as the details of the betrayal become part of a new reality during the recovery process. Numbing is an adaptive tool for surviving unbearable pain, and it's usually comforting to know that it doesn't last. The antidote to numbness helps you to experience and verbalize your emotions because the first step towards a trauma recovery is to experience your feelings. It's another necessary step for the relationship to grow to accept your partner's faults.

The reason the betrayed partner can reject speeding up the recovery process is not difficult to understand. Yet seeking to halt any more disclosure and resistance to learn and experiences details of affair discourage the painful healing cycle.

Hyperarousal

Long after the betrayal has been exposed, people are super-sensitive and super-alert. Their nervous system is overdriven and ready to respond to any more attacks. The deceived partner experiences hyperactivity like a high-speed car engine. Just as one tap on the gas pedal is required for rapid acceleration, a small incident is enough to increase the pulse and reactivate the sweat drums. Through unreasonable behavior and being over-defensive, reasonable acts of self-preservation are distorted. The facts are double-checked and become a full-time problem.

Physiological Hyperarousal

Reaction transforms into overreaction. Disordered sleep becomes routine, as it can be challenging to fall asleep or get up in the morning. Additional signs of hyperarousal are irritability, outbreaks causing trouble. Betrayed partners are easily appalled by ringing telephones, dropped lenses, and the sound of children crying or even playing. Carolyn, who was also a member of the church, found out that her husband Chas had an affair with her church member Roxie, but she still went to prayer while experiencing hyperarousal. She was so nervous she feared she'd leap her skin out. She had trouble falling asleep and then waking up in the morning. She was sleeping in the morning and wouldn't get out of her room. If the alarm clock rattled or a door abruptly opened, she had intense and shocking reactions. Carolyn couldn't concentrate on anything for a long time. Finally, she took one week off the job because she couldn't work properly and returned after two months on a part-time basis. Her family doctor prescribed medications for anxiety, and she began to have intermittent suicidal thoughts. Her depression was deepened. Within a few weeks, her daily counseling antidepressants led to improved mood.

Your psychological state, anxiety and depression can have a strong impact on your appetite. While Carolyn was still one of those who used to stress-eat during stressful times, she lost her appetite. She said, "Although I don't feel slim, I have lost weight. Anxiety over the possible loss of a healthy relationship adversely affects your ability to eat. I have seen people dropping 15 pounds in a month when stressed or struck with the trauma of finding their partner's affair when they have been unsuccessful for many years to lose weight.

HOW TO STOP THE PAIN

Deciding that you are ready to heal is the number one way you end the pain you are experiencing. Actively pursuing healing and committing to feeling better is the key. It is in your commitment to yourself that you will find peace. Show up for yourself every day. Commit and recommit to working through the healing process as many times as you need to. Let go of any beliefs you hold about what needs to happen for you to heal.

These are simply thoughts that keep you distracted from healing. You do not need an apology. You do not need closure. Your healing is your responsibility alone. You are not some passive, powerless victim, waiting for words or actions from someone else to feel better. Once you decide to heal from heartbreak, every action you take will support that decision.

Be courageous. Healing is hard work. Your ex and your breakup, though painful, are very familiar to you. Stepping into the unknown can be scary, but you are not bound to your past. Your breakup is now a part of your past. Heal yourself by refusing to look backward. We are living in the present, always moving forward. Your joy is here and now, and all we have is this moment.

Pro tip: I'm a crier. If I'm really upset, I can get all worked up and start crying. I once found myself just sitting and sobbing about my breakup. I was sitting in my room crying so much, just feeling very sad and miserable, and then the thought hit me. Here I was alone in my house. No one was there physically harming me. My ex was not on the other end of the phone saying anything to me. No nasty text messages were being sent. The only reason I was crying was due to the thoughts in my mind. I was replaying old conversations or imagining my ex being happy somewhere without me. I was sad about something that had happened in the past or things that I didn't even know to be true. I now realized that I could stop crying. I could shift the focus of those thoughts and focus solely on what was currently happening, which was nothing. There was no tangible reason for me to be crying about those things. So I just stopped. I pushed all of those thoughts of old conversations and old things that had happened out of my mind. The next time you find yourself all worked up and crying about your ex, take a moment and access what is happening around you. Suppose you are physically safe and just going over past events or future events that you don't even know to be true. You have the power to just stop.

Breathe and place your focus somewhere else.

Engage yourself with things that give you back some sense of power and control over your life. The following steps were essential to my healing process. After I made the conscious decision to heal my broken heart, these activities renewed my sense of purpose and allowed me to focus on something more than just heartache.

Find a good feeling and chase it.

Ask yourself: what makes you feel good? If the answer to this question comes easily, then go and find that thing and do it. If the answer doesn't come to you as easily, then it is time to do some inner work and exploration. The world is vast, and there are many things you can experiment with and learn that will give you a feeling of joy and peace. It can be simple as taking a walk in the woods or as challenging as completing a 10k and feeling accomplished. During this time, be careful not to engage in risky habits that might feel good at the time but end up jeopardizing your mental and physical health.

The Pleasures of Small Things

There is always a joy, even though it doesn't feel like it right now. Remember the simple pleasures you take pleasure in, such as reading a good book or laughing with a friend. There is a lot to be said about losing yourself in the pages of a good book or preparing yourself a delicious meal on a Sunday afternoon. Even if you're not a great chef, find a recipe and spend some time with yourself cooking something delicious. Make it lovely, and enjoy what you've accomplished. Keep track of the memories you create when doing the little things you love, and go back to them from time to time.

Make time

Make time for yourself, even if it's just a little thing. Make it something you can anticipate. I used to go for a walk around my neighborhood on a regular basis. It might seem insignificant, but getting something to look forward to will help you feel better in the middle of a traumatic situation. So, as part of my quest for ways to lift my spirits, I planned this stroll. I chose a lovely Saturday afternoon and resolved to walk as far as I could for an hour before turning around. I arranged the time and what I would wear, and I resolved to take the time to be thankful for every blessing in my life as I walked. I resolved to devote the hour to appreciate all of the positive things in this world and in my own life. I started to realize that life was still healthy, full, and beautiful as I walked. Even though I was in pain at the time, it was evident that the seasons were always shifting as they had throughout my life.

Volunteer yourself

Volunteering yourself is another excellent way to boost your self-esteem and reintroduce joy into your life. Volunteering has been shown to improve your self-confidence, self-esteem, and overall life satisfaction. It has the potential to positively affect your society while also assisting you in brushing up on your social skills by introducing you to new people. You may also do small-scale volunteer work, such as assisting a friend or neighbor in need. I once volunteered with a group that made lunch bags and distributed them to people in need one afternoon. It was enjoyable to meet new people and concentrate on small tasks such as making sandwiches. It was minor in terms of effort and time commitment, but the gratitude I received from the recipients of those lunches was overwhelming. Volunteering reminded me that I am needed in this world and that I have the power to change things.

Look for ways to make a difference in your neighborhood.

Set a Goal

Having a goal to accomplish helps tremendously to take your mind off of your relationship status. What are those things you would like to accomplish but never had the time to do? Now is your chance. Goals are a part of our long-term vision for our lives. Goals help us define where it is we are going. Once we establish that vision for ourselves, we can then align our actions towards that end goal. Goals are vital. They create markers in our lives. Do you want a life that happens at random? Or do you want to live your life by design? If you answered by design, then now is the perfect time to firmly place those goals in your mind and work towards them. You are capable of achieving greatness, even at this moment. Even though things might feel bleak, you got this! There are so many great moments and achievements still out there waiting for you. All you need is the willingness to dedicate the time to your goals and a bit of persistence, and you will get there.

Good things rarely just happen to people at random; you must make a plan, figure out a way to make it happen, and be consistent. Remember that you've got a real good shot at some pretty great things, especially right now. So sign up for that course, train for that race, maybe even write that book. Channel everything you've got into your goals and makes yourself proud!

PHASES OF HEALING FROM A BROKEN HEART

It has been said that although heartbreak is a medical condition, unfortunately, there is no medical treatment to cure the broken heart. Of course, there are pills to increase your heart function, prevent heart attack, or calm you down temporarily. Many brokenhearted people went to drug dealers to escape from the heartbreak, but instead of freeing themselves from the emotion, they became addicted to drugs. It is like getting rid of a headache by being attached to aspirin. What is the meaning of running from one attachment to another attachment?

Scientists and mystics, or psychologists and spiritualists, are not in line with many topics. However, they agree that forgiveness (and letting go) is the cure for a broken heart.

They argued that forgiving a wrongdoer would release the resentment in the heart and normalize the hormone responsible for depression. It is a gradual process, and as with many other illnesses, healing commonly takes more time than the coming of the illness. It is so because forgiving is not happened merely by saying "I forgive you" because it is not directly about the wrongdoer; it is more about us. In other words, forgiveness is more about forgiving ourselves than forgiving others.

Forgiveness requires a deep understanding of what is going on in our heads. It involves learning, unlearning, and relearning the lessons that love gives you. It takes courage to change our values and beliefs. It invites you to change your perspectives in seeing your experience. While living the process, you should not allow yourself to please your wounds like scratching the itch. It is like a doctor suggesting you avoid ice cream during the process of curing your toothache. There is no shortcut to healing a broken heart. Drugs are the shortcuts that will lead you back to heartbreak. Suicide is, of course, the worst shortcut that will heal you from everything, including healing you from life.

You need to unlearn and relearn the experience because you were "dumb" and "blind" when you were in love. You were irrational, uncritical, and careless while falling in love. As your critical mind returns and you become aware of your values and importance, you will be ready to let go of things that no longer serve you for goodness.

There are quite a lot of paths to forgive and let go of for the healing process, some of them are case-specific, and some others are universal. Here, I have outlined for you the steps of healing a broken heart by forgiving and letting go that I believe can work in various cases, especially in the romantic theme. But first, to encourage you to take the step, I will share with you a brief historical (and scientific) background of what we are talking about.

Forgiveness has been long known as an effective treatment for various mental-caused illnesses or psychosomatics, including medical heartbreak. Although spiritualists and mystics recognized it from ancient times, forgiveness becomes a therapy model (Forgiveness Therapy), which is associated with a professor of educational psychology at the University of Wisconsin-Madison, Robert Enright, Ph.D.

It is reported that the first empirical study on the healing effects of forgiveness conducted by Enright was in 1989. However, in 1993, Enright published forgiveness (as a therapy model), consisting of four phases. It took only two years that forgiveness therapy absorbed many researchers' attention. From 1995 to 1999, Enright's forgiveness therapy was discussed, studied, examined, and brewed so that it went matured and popular. In 1999, due to his model popularity, Enright was crowned by the most respected magazine in the world, Time, as the Forgiveness Trailblazer.

Interestingly, it is said that Enright had never used the term forgiveness therapy in his initial work. However, today, a Google search for that term turns up 14,800,000 results, and it is amazing.

Enright's model consists of four phases: the uncovering phase, the decision phase, the work phase, and the deepening phase. I will describe and enrich them with some spiritual and philosophical advice to deepen the meaning and strengthen the effect of each phase. I don't want to be different, but without something new and empowering, this discussion is not useful compared to what the researchers have to say about them.

The best way to run Forgiveness Therapy is with assistance from a therapist (psychotherapist or hypnotherapist). However, although it may take more time, self-treatment is also enough. The reason why forgiveness needs to be assisted is that we usually experience internal conflict during the process. In other words, it is usual to fight ourselves back because there must be a part within us that won't forgive people and won't let go of resentments. We will see that in a second.

The Uncovering Phase

The heartbreak experience holds a lot of strength hidden or suppressed in the unconscious mind. Since we are uncritical to what our perceptions received during falling in love and broken heart, many environmental or self-suggestion suggestions bypassed the conscious mind and went directly to the unconscious mind. These suggestions play double roles; they strengthen the heartbreak experience (amplify the mental and medical effect), and they can also weaken the experience and allow us to let go. In this phase, you bring up the strength onto the conscious mind so that you can make significant changes and gain your power back.

The hardest part in this phase is to take a different perspective in evaluating the experience, especially without assistance. During the heartbreak experience, you are standing on the experiencer perspective. If you want to evaluate the experience critically, you must take the observer's perspective. In other words, you are required to take a distance from yourself as the experiencer; and that is tough.

Imagine that you are taking all the files from the drawers and put them on the desk. Those files are the unconscious reason why you fell in love with that person. What you expected from that person, what made you disappointed, how it affects your life (physical and mental), what lesson you can learn from that experience, what benefits you can get if you stop experiencing it, and so on. All of these files are learned, and some of them are unlearned. Also, you need to relearn what you once learned to be a happy person. You will only be able to work on all of these files if you stand from the observer's perspective.

Without being an objective observer, your response to the question "why you fell in love with her" will be, "I don't know... I love her very much... just it." However, suppose you are objective in evaluating your experience. In that case, you may say, "Well, she is beautiful and has a nice body..." and then you learn this lesson: she is not the only beautiful girl with a nice body around you. A part of you may respond back, "I know it. But I only love her..." then you return to the initial question. You don't want to run around the endless fight within yourself, so you must take the lesson since you don't want to be in that situation forever. Some people may say, "It is fine to be like this. I believe that one day she will return to me and regret that she has broken my heart." I must say that it is just wishful thinking. "Who tells you that she will return?", "Don't you know what effects this experience gives you?" and some other critical questions to make you conscious of what you are currently experiencing.

The process of the uncovering phase is not linear but recursive. You will jump to the answers to different questions to answer one question. You will need to return to the previous questions or jump to the next questions to gather the answers to understand your goal. Although it is a recursive process, it is not endless. It is like recursively filling all the glasses with water until they are full. When all glasses are full, all questions are answered, the uncovering phase is completed.

The Decision Phase

As you pass the uncovering phase, you may now have a long list of reasons to forgive the person who broke your heart. It is also reasonable to feel it too hard to forgive; none said that having your heart broken is easy. However, if you look at the reason to forgive them objectively, it just does not make sense to keep the anger, sadness, or resentment in your heart for those who are jeopardizing your physical and mental health.

If you find it difficult to forgive, be advised that, like heartbreak, forgiveness is also a process. A hypnotherapist, Mike Mandel, advised that we need to forgive first, then the emotion (of forgiveness) will follow. It means that the time you decide to forgive is not necessarily the time you forgive completely.

The decision phase requires you to decide whether to forgive or not. It is fine if you still feel anger and offense, but those feelings should not prevent you from forgiving. If it is still challenging to decide to forgive, you can make a list of the pros and cons of your forgiving action. See the list objectively and find the reasons you have in the uncovering phase to fight the cons list. Imagine how you will feel if you no longer hold the wounds in your heart; forgive. Remember also forgiveness is not a gift you present to the person who broke your heart but to you alone. Honestly, people who broke your heart do not deserve to be forgiven, but you do. You deserve a calm mind, a peaceful heart, a healthy body, and happier life.

The process you have gone through in the uncovering phase is actually telling you that you must make only one rational decision. The decision is to forgive them. You may now say, "Ok, I forgive her!" but you still feel the pain. You still feel so because you don't come to the work phase yet. However, as you decide to forgive her, healing starts to take place. The process will speed up and be amplified during the work phase. Again, forgiveness is not a spontaneous healing process, but it can be faster than healing physical wounds.

The Work Phase

We have different types of relationships with other people. We are with our family (spouse and children) more frequently than with our friends. Sometimes, we meet our friends more frequently than our romantic partners. Some relationships last for years (friendship, romantic love), and some other relationships last forever (marriage, unless divorced) and until death do us part (parents and their children). While a relationship determines the frequency of interaction and how long we will be together, anyone in our circles (family, romantic partner, and friendship) can break our hearts. Moreover, the way we forgive them is different from one type to another type of relationship.

How you forgive your children or spouse is different from how you forgive your friends or romantic partner. If your children (one of them) break your heart, you need to forgive them by letting them know that you forgive their mistakes. Moreover, it would help to correct their behaviors and words so they don't do it again in the future. It is so because you and your children are bound together in a blood relationship. It also applies between you and your brothers and sisters. Your spouse can also be forgiven, but since your relationship is not as eternal as between you and your brothers, sisters, and children, you can take another way to stop having a relationship with them (e.g., by divorce). In that case, you can forgive them without them knowing that you forgive them. This kind of forgiveness (silent forgiveness) applies to romantic and friendship relationships.

Different types of relationships teach us different types of forgiveness. You forgive your brothers, sisters, and children because you love them, while to your friends and romantic partners, you forgive because you love yourself. The first interprets forgiveness as "giving," while the second interprets forgiveness as "releasing." By forgiving your children, you give them a chance to be better persons tomorrow while you don't expect anything from your partner who has broken your heart; what you really want is to release the mental toxins from yourself no matter what they will be in the future (you don't care). And, of course, this opinion is open to be criticized.

There is a "release of mental toxins" when you forgive your family, but it is a different story, and I don't want to go in that. Since we are discussing forgiveness in a romantic context, what I am going to say is all about releasing the mental toxins within us without letting them know that we forgive them. We also don't care about what they will be tomorrow. Of course, we pray for their goodness, but we also know that they will be out of our control. Even, we don't have to return to them and put them in the special position where they were for it means that we give them a chance to break our hearts again. Therefore, releasing in this case, almost eliminates them from our circle and erases the data associated with them in our brains. It sounds like "I forgive you, and goodbye."

The work phase is about neutralizing the emotions of the memories associated with the person who has broken our hearts and setting up new boundaries that exclude them from the circle. Without having the emotional association neutralized, each memory will likely bleed the almost-healed wounds again. Without excluding them from our circle, they will likely break our hearts again. In this phase, the unlearning, learning, and relearning of the thinking and behavioral patterns occur.

Two works need to be done in this phase: mental work and physical work. The mental work includes unlearning old thinking patterns and learning new ones, and the physical work includes the Emotional Freedom Technique (EFT).

Having these works combined together, the neutralization of emotion and self-empowerment will certainly fall into place. The original Forgiveness Therapy by Enright didn't include EFT, and I decided to make small changes in it, for I found it works all the time. I got the knowledge to modify the forgiveness therapy from

MENTAL AND PHYSICAL WORK

Mental Work

You have the power until you decide to forgive the person who has broken your heart. Nonetheless, the power is worthless unless you put it to good use. The healing process has already begun, and by doing these mental exercises, you can hasten and intensify the results. These are the mental exercises you must complete.

Either in the morning or evening, you need to put yourself in a very relaxing state. You can sit on the backed chair or lying down on the bed. The best times to do this are either when you want to go to sleep or just wake up from your sleep. These times are said the best because, in these times, our mind is in the alpha state, which is required to make changes at the subconscious level.

After reaching the relaxed state, recall only the positive memories associated with the person. If the negative memories intrude in, don't push them away but place them with the positive ones side by side. See them in different "screens" in your mind; let's call them positive and negative screens. Ask yourself if you want to pay more attention to the positive screen. As you pay attention to the positive screen, you know that the screen turns more vivid, the colors go more saturated while the negative screen is automatically dimmed, and the color turns to grey. Intentionally feel the emotion as you watch the moments projected on the positive screen. While having the positive emotion from the positive screen, in your mind, say "you are a good person, thank you" twice or three times until you feel the emotion internalized in your body.

In case that the negative screen pops up frequently, it is a sign that the subconscious mind is calling you to work on that screen. It is not a barrier to healing, and it is a chance to heal. While watching on the negative screen, you will probably revive the negative emotion, but you can take the observer's perspective. It is normal if you feel pain because it goes up to be released. If you press them down, you tend to keep them inside your subconscious mind, and that is definitely the wrong way to heal your broken heart.

Bring your mind into a "learning mode" and look at the screen without emotionally judging what you are looking at and feeling. Supply material to your subconscious mind to learn. Tell these to yourself. "She is a good person, and she is not perfect. She made a mistake because she is not perfect. She is just a human like me. I can make the same mistake. Perhaps, she is hurt inside. Perhaps, she was grown in a painful environment. I am the one responsible for my heart. I am healing. Therefore, I forgive her and leave her." Tell these several times until you feel better since your subconscious mind unlearns the old thinking patterns (e.g., she didn't love me, I am unworthy, I loved her too much, etc.). Don't be sticky to the sequence of the sentences. The important points are the meaning of the sentences that you want your subconscious mind to learn. When the meanings are changed, internalized, and associated with the moments projected on the negative screen, your emotion will also change based on the Law of Emotion.

When emotional changes occur within you, it is easier for you to dim and blur the pictures projected on the negative screen. You can do that intentionally; dim the screen, blur the picture, make it less and less saturated, narrow the screen, and let the screen go in the darkness of your mind.

Having worked on the negative screen, you can recall the positive screen and intentionally make it more vivid, saturated, wide, and close. Allow yourself to feel a positive emotion and affirm that "you are a good person, thank you" and, if needed, add "and goodbye." Nevertheless, you can push the positive screen away as you did with the negative screen. You need neutral emotion so that when you meet the person in the future, there is no way to feel the negative emotion anymore, and you don't have to fall in love with them again. Remember this! You don't need to give them a second chance, but you also don't have to create enmity with them. The feeling of hostility is a sign that there are still negative leftovers in your heart. If any, repeat the work. For some people, doing this mental work by themselves is not easy. If you find it difficult to do it by yourself, you can get assistance from a hypnotherapist.

What you just have done was unlearning the old thinking patterns and learning the new ones. You also relearned the positive thinking patterns associated with that person. These are all taught in Enright's model of forgiveness, with a slight difference in the description. By doing these mental works alone, you can heal in several days. In order to speed it up and amplify the effects, you need to do the physical work.

Physical Work

It is no longer a secret that emotions are generated and distributed within our bodies. Psychologists once maintained that a part in the brain called the limbic system is the only agent responsible for emotion. Still, today they have discovered that emotion is an orchestra that involves the brain, the heart, and the body. Since emotion is like what they said, working with the body can promote, speed up, and amplify the effects that we expect from working with the brain or the mind.

Emotion has also been unofficially defined as "energy of motion," where the "e" stands for "energy." It says that emotion makes us move, either approaching or avoiding something or someone; it is related to motivation. In Traditional Chinese Medicine (TCM), emotion is understood as the effect of the energy they call Chi. Chi is a term that is usually interpreted as pure energy or life energy. The discipline of Chi training is called Qigong, and the practitioner can be called "energy workers." While I am not trying to go into that thing, it is interesting to see how the "energy workers" understand emotion.

The energy workers understand emotions as the mental symptoms reflecting the quality of the energy flow present in the body; they also know that the quality of the energy flow influences physical and mental health. Negative emotions are the "effects" of the poor quality in the energy flow, and positive emotions are the "effects" of the good quality of the energy flow.

The chi flows within the body through channels known as meridians. The human body also has three energy centers where the chi is stored and distributed to the overall body parts. The quality of the chi flow is influenced by several things, including physical injuries and mental processing.

How could the mental processing influence the chi? It is so because, as TCM knows, where the mind goes, there the chi flows.

The three energy centers (called dantiens) are said to play different roles. The lower dantien (located right below the belly button) is responsible for physical survival; the middle dantien (located in the heart or the center of the chest) is responsible for feeling; the upper dantien (located in the brain) is responsible for thought and imagination.

The chi flows through the meridian channels that connect the three energy centers. When the channels experience blockage either by physical or mental factors, the quality of chi flow decreases so that the physical and mental imbalances occur. Since these energy centers are wired altogether, blockage in one area will disturb the flow quality in the other areas.

Overthinking occurs in mind, and it can disturb the meridian in the brain or head. Heartbreak occurs in the heart, and it can disturb the meridian in the chest. Suppose we relate this to what psychology has to say about Takotsubo Cardiomyopathy (the heartbreak syndrome). In that case, we can have the big picture of why overthinking can worsen the feeling of heartbreak and why it can harm our physical and mental health. We also know that what we think determines what we feel; the meaning our mind gives to something, someone, or an event determines the emotion we have toward them. By looking at the big picture, we become aware that we are looking at emotion processing which happens in multiple layers.

Now, the essential thing to know is how to unblock the meridian channels to increase the quality of the chi flow. Acupuncture is well known in TCM and is now applied in many places in the world to unblock the meridian channels. Nevertheless, it is not available for all people, especially to those who are fearful of needles. Fortunately, it is not the only way to physically unblock the blocked meridians. The easiest way to do the work is by tapping on certain points in the body. This method is now applied on many occasions and has been proven as an effective method. Psychotherapists and hypnotherapists worldwide have used this method to help their clients get rid of psychosomatic emotional turmoil. They named this method Emotion Freedom Technique or EFT, but the origin was TCM.

Tapping on different points will give different physical and mental effects for different points are responsible for different purposes. Mike Mandel, a master of hypnotherapist and NLP, has pointed out six or seven meridian points responsible for forgiveness by adopting EFT. Mandel advised us that we need to verbally state some affirmations while tapping on the points; I prepared them below. If you do this work before or after the mental work I prescribed above, your healing process will speed up, and the effects will be amplified significantly. It is true because you work and heal in multiple layers.

These are the points that Mike Mandel pointed for you:

Tapped points and affirmation:

1. At the center-top of the head; tapping with the point and middle fingers 21 seconds while affirming "I release the old energy and unblock the energy flow";

2. At the center-vertical line in the forehead; tapping with the four fingers except for thumb 21 seconds while affirming, "I release my negative thoughts because I don't need it anymore";

3. At the outer side of the eyes; tapping with the point and middle fingers 21 seconds while affirming, "I choose positive thoughts because it empowers me";

4. Below the eyes; tapping with the point and middle fingers 21 seconds while affirming, "I release all resentments, sadness, and sorrows for I no longer need them";

5. Above the chest; tapping with the point and middle fingers 21 seconds while affirming, "I release the negative feelings and replace with positive feelings… I choose positive feelings… I am happy";

6. Hold the wrist gently (either right or left; it is recommended to hold the tapping hand) for 21 seconds while affirming "I have full control over what I feel";

7. On the back of the hand, the space between the little and ring finger; tapping with the point and middle fingers 21 seconds while affirming, "I choose positivity, I choose happiness, I release all negativities within me, I am healing myself";

It is important to know how to do this correctly.

1. It is advisable that you do this physical work after doing the mind works we discussed before.

2. It is recommended that you do this physical work while standing on your feet so that the energy can flow freely to your soles and be grounded into the earth;

3. It is not recommended to tap the points more than 50 seconds for it can overload yourself with energy;

4. It is not recommended to tap the points hard for it can damage your tissues;

5. State the affirmation with confidence;

6. State the affirmation several times until you feel the emotional change in your heart;

Silent your body after all the works to feel the mild vibration rushing your body. The energy takes care of your body. You must keep your mind away from inviting any negativity you have dispelled in the mental work.

Although these works' emotional and physical effects are magical, the works are not magic but scientific. Since these are not magic, they take time. Just do it and believe that it works. Mike Mandel said, "it works no matter you believe it or not." Do these works (physical and mental works) regularly and trust the process.

Forgiveness therapy does not stop here. It is important to contemplate the constructive changes after doing the works. The more we find the positive changes within us, the more we heal. It means that the effect can be deepened (after speed up and amplified). That's what the deepening phase is about.

The Deepening Phase

Even in the first or second time doing the work phase, you will have experienced an emotional change; you will have felt better. However, the deepening phase is supposed to be done after having the work phase done for some time (at least seven times/a week) so that you can be sure that what you have done in a week was effective. In my mind, you can also do the deepening phase after the 3rd night so that you can take certain actions to deepen the effect as soon as possible.

The heart of the deepening phase is the contemplation of your achievement in the work phase. You can refer to your mental and physical state to count your achievements through the work phase. Here are some of the general mental and physical changes you may experience after having the work phase done. Some changes are not mentionable, for they may be personal and case-specific.

Mental changes:

1. You become more mindful;

2. Your ability to focus on what you are doing returns;

3. Your motivation to work returns;

4. Your critical thinking ability returns;

5. You feel happier and more positive;

6. Colors and shapes are seen clearer;

7. Small pieces of beautiful objects or scenes are enjoyable to you;

8. Your need to sleep lessened (your sleep cycle returns to normal);

9. Your sleep quality increases;

10. You are calmer;

11. You become more social;

12. Comedies and simple jokes make you laugh;

13. Your emotion to anything associated with her returns neutral;

14. You no longer expect anything from her as you have set a new boundary that excludes her from the circle;

15. It is easier to let go of things you cannot control.

Physical changes:

1. You become more active physically;

2. You breathe deeper and slower;

3. Your body feels "lighter" and relaxed;

4. Your chest feels relieved;

5. Your muscles strength returns;

6. Your skin turns brighter and smoother;

7. You smile more often;

8. You become healthier.

As you heal, you may experience some of them, all of them, or more than what I have listed above. Whatever experience unlisted above must be positive, for any healing gives you all positive changes mentally and physically. Among the changes, the 13th mental change and the 8th physical change are clear signs that your heart is healed (the work phase really works).

In the deepening phase, you are required to list the positive changes you experience mentally and physically. After checking the list, you are recommended to deepen the effects or changes by practicing gratitude. In spiritual teachings, gratitude is another way to pray for more than the goodness you have received, and there is nothing wrong with that as long as you ask God. It will help you to direct or focus more on the positive changes. As your mind is "busy" to focus on the positive, you heal not only the wounds but also the scars.

You can also take physical work as your new habit. You can practice the physical work regularly, although you are not experiencing heartbreak anymore. What you need to do is just adjust the affirmation based on your current needs.

This is the last phase of "modified" Forgiveness Therapy. Forgiveness Therapy teaches us that we have no choice but to forgive and let go if we want to heal the broken heart. We should not cling to things that we cannot control, and one of them is "being loved as we expect"; we should love ourselves more, for it is always with us while other people will come and certainly go.

FORGIVING AND MOVING FORWARD

Forgiveness is not a single event. It is a step-by-step process of letting go with an open heart and tackling your anger correctly. If you had already found any salvation, you would not have gone so far as to start the healing process. It is out of touch with the reality if you choose to forgive too early, without tending to your wounds and scars caused by the betrayal. Your profound wounds and sufferings, while still fresh and you still in the aftershock of betrayal, yet you propose forgiveness too early. You have to be free from anger and resentment when you start to establish security, willingness, and compassionate communication. As you search for the meaning in your life's events together, you will come to be more empathetic. While forgiveness is not a prerequisite of recovery, it is necessary for complete healing. Now is the time to make a conscious decision to seek forgiveness or to grant it. It is time to forgive shattered expectations and start to rebuild your relationship in meaningful ways. No more surprises are welcomed. And no more shoes should drop after forgiveness has been granted. The full extent of betrayal and all the essential details should be discussed and resolved by now. Forgiveness is necessary if an attempt has been made to change from any or both partners. For example, dysfunctional couples work on their issues in counseling or in a support group, such as for addiction, codependence, or trauma from the past. The steps that lead to granting forgiveness are strictly parallel to the steps for trauma recovery. You have to build a bridge for forgiveness while following the model of recovery for healing from trauma. The positive experiences will slowly open your hearts to each other. By every thoughtful gesture, every session of careful listening, and every attempt to consider each other's perspective, you will affirm the compassion and respect that are the essential preconditions for reconciliation.

I see people stuck in denial or retaliation. After Oren had finished his affair and disposed of the futon on which he had physical relations with another woman, Olivia wasn't sure she could forgive Oren. Olivia said, "I'm supposed to forgive you and get through it because you and your mistress are so great in so many ways. What disturbs me is that I feel obligated to forgive him. Why are his feelings more important than mine? The meaning of forgiveness confused Olivia. Like many others, she felt that forgiving Oren would message that she was fine with what he had done. She was scared that it would be easy for him to betray her again if she forgave him go too easily. She sometimes had a strong feeling of vengeance, wanting to make him suffer as she did. She even thought of having an affair herself. It's possible to attain a functional stage of recovery without forgiveness, but it's impossible to achieve the ultimate healing for yourself or your relationship without forgiveness.

The best gift you can give to yourself is forgiveness. You can make substantial progress in your life's journey if you can free yourself from the anguish and burden of the past by forgiving. You can start the next chapter of your life with self-confidence and more options than you had before. It is an option to forgive. You chose not to be taken hostage by the events that have happened in the past. Authentic forgiveness accepts the damage and is the product of deliberate practice for evolving.

Forgiveness is a Process

Forgiveness is based on the sincere remorse from the betraying partner from the couple who heal together. Both are involved equally. Over time, you have made your intent to reconcile clear and have shown commitment to each other (through specific acts of nurturing relationships).

Forgiveness is letting go of emotional bitterness, resentment and grudges. Forgiveness is based on a sincere intent to release anger and resentment and a conscious decision to move your life forward. Forgiveness is freeing the suffering. Forgive, and you free yourself, minimizing any injury from the continuous pain of trauma. Forgiveness is a personal act that affects your life's consistency directly. Forgiveness lets you let go of vengeance. You consciously decide not to blame anyone but rather to live in an environment full of solutions. Rachel searched for ways to let Ralph know that she was focused and intended on forgiving him and loving him. She told herself repeatedly that she had a massive gift and she should not mention Lara's name or any event from her past that she thought might embarrass him.

- The Personal Benefits of Forgiveness

It fosters your well-being by forgiving others. You get focused, free of grudges and pain, as you begin to let go of the idea of punishing and taking revenge. Anger release in a constructive way allows serenity to fill your life. by forgiving, You move from being a victim to a survivor. Forgiveness frees you from the tyranny of others and past incidents and eliminates the risk of misdirecting your frustration towards other relationships. How great it is to choose yourself as the master of your life, then being a prisoner of the past, your thoughts and circumstances! Forgiveness is beneficial for your emotional and physical health. The Stanford Forgiveness project has demonstrated how to eradicate the aggravation and anger of grudges by educating people. The forgiveness cycle reduces significant risk factors for heart disease, stroke, and other serious diseases (stress, frustration, and depression) and higher blood pressure. Increased immune function, reduced other health problems such as headaches, stomach aches and dizziness, heart palpitations can be achieved by forgiving people. Forgive for your emotional and physical health.

Many who have learned to forgive have strengthened their emotional, mental and spiritual functions. It increases hope, optimism, and the possibility that an improved solution view will be created. The substitution of positive-negative emotions improves the ability to feel linked, trusted, and loved.

- Are Some Things Unforgivable?

Some affairs are both unacceptable and challenging to try to forgive. You must ensure your security first. Forgiveness of unlawful conduct is like canceling a debt paid off on a bad check. It's also hard to forgive someone without remorse, if not impossible. Excuses must be sincere, and action must be supporting those excuses. Alcoholics, gamblers and thugs often feel guilty on the spot and promise to change, but then do the same. Forgiving a recurring criminal who has a very self-centric or carefree behavior does not make much sense unless you protect yourself from further injury by removing yourself from the relationship.

Betrayed partners and unfaithful partners must decide whether to forgive and move forward or leave without having closure. If the affair lasted too long, and the infidel partner is not compassionate, it may not be possible to overlook his actions and mistakes. If any disillusionment accompanying the affair has lasted for too long, and if the infidel partner cannot take responsibility for fixing issues, reconciliation with such partner is unlikely.

Is There a Right Time to Forgive?

Too long to forgive may strengthen your despair and hopelessness. On the other hand, premature or inadequate forgiveness may provide a falsely same sense of healing. Too quickly, forgiveness can lessen your self-esteem and often empower proper forgiveness. Forgiveness is made with a grudge because it's "the right thing to do" or because it is "the right one." Forgiveness that is not sincere or genuine only creates more intimate and honest communication.

- Forgiving Too Soon

A standard error is that it wants to get away too soon from pain and anger. In a few weeks, the unfaithful partner saw the wrong way, confessed some transgressions, and was ready to end the unfaithfulness. This "flight into the health" is supported by a training partner anxious to overcome the pressure of the crisis. Perhaps they agree that the infidelity was a little bump on the road, or maybe a boulder, but the guilty party excused itself, which is the end. The easy forgiveness of hurtful behavior can be perceived as a license. Such denial and superficiality may reflect how a couple has carried out their entire relationship.

- Beware of Pseudo-forgiveness

Either or both partners can enthusiastically embrace a kind of pseudo-forgiveness to spare the discomfort of the confrontation. You can't argue that unfaithfulness never happened. Race to fast solutions perpetuates skepticism rather than an actual resolution. Forgiveness, which feels like a fast-food drive, can lead to long but deep resentment. Neither spouse profits from pseudo-forgiveness. This can also build a continuous loop of rebellion accompanied by apologies. Sadly, some unfaithful partners measure distrust's cost-benefit ratio, undergo no fucking, and continue the cycle. To experience the thrill of forbidden love, they will pay the costs of a brief disappointment. Many people seek to get forgiveness after having been allowed before the incident.

- Lingering Suspicion

It is time to ask what else happens if a couple has been working during the entire recovery stages for many months. Nothing alleviates the suffering of the trained partner! If a betrayed partner doesn't respond, a stubborn and well-meaning partner's efforts to have good faith may be concerned that the unfaithful partner remains ambivalent or that infidelity goes on a secret. Spouses also have a responsive "radar" for their partner's continued presence even though the company seems to be over outside observers. You can't continue without being safe, and you can't forgive. The dangerous partner can only remain defensive and alert to every hint of attack if the risk for re-injury is real and imminent. A deceived spouse who responds as if the matter is still alive and well and right (i.e., not over) has reason to be obsessed and hyper-survived. Suppose the current case ends, but there is no reasonable assurance against future infidelity. In that case, it prevents the treated partner from being unprepared for the next act of treason to stay stuck in unmitigated suffering.

- Reverberating Pain from the Past

After the matter has undoubtedly ended and the unfaithful party has made honest efforts to amend it, they can react to more than the subject. In the life of the betrayed partner, the affair can reawaken unresolved injuries. The case is proof to some disaster partners that the planet was born a cruel and unequal place to suffer. Their families or previous relationships may have mistreated them and harmed them. Exploring the relationship history of an unremittingly injured partner can reveal infidelity by parental figures, exploitation of or sexual abuse by trustworthy adults, bullying of the peer group, etc.

Georgia was so angry and prolonged over George's daily coffee breaks with a young coworker that it seemed an extreme over-reaction. Georgia understood George's rejuvenation from sexual innuendos and lively talks. She acknowledged his point that sex or secure emotional connection had not been there. He also acknowledged that their marital relationship was focused on love and companionship, but he knew that George had ended any interaction with his "mate." However, Georgia has been physically aggressive on several occasions and threatened to end the marriage, despite this understanding. She refused to console and reassure her George's efforts. He drove away for hours in his car when she was sarcastic and brutal to him. The history of Georgia's family revealed that it was still very bitter for a younger woman thirty years earlier that she was still very sharp about her father's desertion. Once she found out that George had spent so much time with another woman, it unleashed her clear lack of faith in Menand's love-hate for his dad. They both were so miserable George and Georgia that they negotiated a truce at long last. She accepted no verbal or physical attack on him. He agreed that he would stay and listen to others if she said she hurt without screaming and yelling. They grew nearer as Georgia shared their fears with him. She asked him to pardon her constant cruelty, and he asked her to forgive her for violating her confidence and opening old wounds. Most couples recover over time, like George and Georgia. However, if the tone of marriage continues to be retribution and retribution, the union cannot obtain the necessary incentive for healing.

- Accusatory Suffering

It must be recognized that the initial desperation of some treated partners is never overcome. They are a living memorial of betrayal, and they continue to blow on their misery's living coals to keep it alive. It may be difficult to understand why betrayed spouses want to sustain suffering by investigating an open wound deliberately. Whenever the wound closes, the wound is poked up again to prevent it from healing. These treacherous partners are like victims of incest and domestic violence who are not allowed to cure their psychic injuries. Accusatory pain is the term used to describe this constant suffering coined by Elizabeth and Arthur Seagull.

Certain people go on their way to an acceptable and understanding approach through this accusatory stage, and others stay forever in this place of punishment. Its unconscious is one of the keys to accusative pain. Unconsciously, the victims believe that the person who hurt them is relieved of the guilt and gets away too quickly by making their full recovery. The wound may look like a small scratch rather than a fatal backstroke if you are no longer pained. They fear they may forget the depth and the extent of their injury unless they continue to suffer. The deceived partner becomes a living monument to treason to avoid this, a vivid statement of pain caused by the unfaithful partner. The irony is that a suspicious partner will respond by having the help of an emotive colleague or acquaintance to a consistent lack of forgiveness and end up crossing the line again. What is the difference if your wife never believes in you anyway? It is not difficult to understand such a lack of hope, but choosing the partner concerned and taking responsibility for their loyalty is not the wounded partner.

- Self-absorbed Unforgiving

Betrayed partners who can forgive are willing to relinquish their role as and see things through their partner's eyes. Tyler illustrates someone who is too self-sustained for compassion and forgiveness in his injury. For nineteen years, he lived and breathed the story of how his wife Tanya, before she married, hurt her with an unforgivable transgression. Why he wounded her was blind. After only three weeks of engagement, Tyler decided he wasn't ready for marriage and broke off their commitment. Tanya was distracted by his dropout and was standing at a bar for one night. It did not matter what happened, and she felt numb. She did not care. After some months, the wedding plans were made, Tyler realized how much he missed her. Tanya admitted to Tyler that she had casual sex with somebody else while separating because she didn't want to have secrets between them. Tyler's reaction was violent and terrifying. His cherished view of her as "pure" has been forever destroyed. During his many years of marriage, he remained angry.

The parents had been hesitant for life and bound by mutual hate and anger. Tanya's "sin" provided the perfect opportunity for Tyler to practice persistent behaviors at home. His inability to pass the 'disloyalty' of Tanya undermined its bond and affected their lives in several ways adversely. First of all, Tyler never invested fully in her marriage, only for failure. The nagging fear that they might be separated by next month was in the back of his mind. He told himself that after having a child, he only stayed until his daughter finished high school. When he softened toward Tanya from time to time, he immediately returned to portray her as a "slut" and felt another fit of righteous indignation. Tanya was never able to forgive himself for doing anything against her principles, so she embraced her eternal punishment. A breakthrough came when Tyler listened for the first time to Tanya, and he heard that his abandonment was responsible for his desperation. He realized that he hurt her, and she suffered so much. His broken commitment was not the only victim! He had been searching for nearly twenty years, enabling himself to feel his suffering. Without the weight of his explanation, he couldn't believe how much happier he felt.

FALLING IN LOVE WITH YOURSELF

Radical Self-Love

We need self-love and self-compassion more than ever in the wake of a breakup or divorce.

It's not your job to love someone else right now; it's just your job to love yourself. In a radical way. With ferocity. Without reservation. You'll feel as if you've never loved yourself before.

We just want to be cherished and cared for, but we refuse to do so for ourselves. Instead, we search for love and someone else to 'complete' us outside of ourselves, oblivious to the fact that our greatest source of love is inside ourselves. Since we are already complete, no one can complete us.

Yes, we want someone to balance us out and add more meaning to our lives, but we don't need them to complete our lives. As previously said, it's never about having attention from the outside – it's always been inside work. All begins with oneself.

Indeed, the lack of self-love can leave us with a bottomless void that another person can never fill. When we don't love ourselves, we are always looking for someone else to do it for us, hoping the unloved part of us will finally feel loved; we are demanding from others the love we aren't giving to ourselves. And we wonder why we don't get it! We are the only ones who can fill that void with self-love.

We are so afraid of being alone that we put up with being disrespected in a relationship; we are so afraid of being abandoned that we end up abandoning ourselves.

What's great about self-love is that it has very feminine energy. It's gentle, soothing and comforting like a loving parent's embrace. It validates our pain and our difficulties. On the other hand, courage gives us the fierce masculine energy that motivates us into action despite our fears and other negative emotions. We need both kindness and fierceness. It's like the yin and the yang.

The greatest achievement is to be yourself in a world that continuously tries to mold you into someone else. (E. E. Cummings)

We hear a lot about self-love these days, however many people aren't sure what it is or how it works in reality, or they believe it's woo-woo and therefore unsuitable for them.

I define self-love as the complete acceptance of things as they are, rather than wishing they were otherwise. Accepting who you are and where you are on your life's path, and by that, I mean all of you and your life, good, poor, and ugly, is part of this.

It's about you accepting yourself for who you are, flaws and all, and building on that solid base to become even stronger, rather than believing there's something wrong with you that you need to 'correct.'

Self-love is the key to living your most amazing life and is the cure that allows you to let go of perfection and release self-judgment. It's also the antidote to your inner critic, and it will set your true self free.

Why is that? Because acceptance is the opposite of judgment. As we saw in chapter five, the inner critic is all about judgment, and it wants to deny rather than accept reality. Its weapons of choice are either obligation and guilt (all your 'should') or fear and self-doubt.

Another big part of acceptance is forgiveness: forgiving yourself and others when things go wrong – and they will – over and over again. (More on this in chapter eight).

The Most Important Relationship

The self-love journey is fundamentally about changing your relationship with yourself. On this journey, you will learn that it is the most important relationship you will ever have in your life.

You are the common denominator in all of your life's ups and downs, and you are with yourself 24 hours a day, seven days a week, when other people come and go.

As a result, don't delegate the burden of being on your own side and unconditionally loving yourself to others. You will feel like you have truly come home to yourself when you realize your self-love is the root of love in your life and give it to yourself no matter what. In reality, loving yourself is akin to coming full circle after searching for love elsewhere, sometimes in the wrong places.

The shepherd boy Santiago in The Alchemist dreamed of a treasure and set out to find it. The treasure he was searching for turned out to be hidden in the ruins where he had the dream in the first place. It had always been there, and all he had to do was rediscover it.

That's how self-love works. You already possess it, and all you need to do now is rediscover it. Isn't this a liberating realization?

My favorite self-compassion specialist Kristin Neff says that self-love is made up of three things if you want to go deeper.

1. Self-kindness

We behave with gentleness and kindness towards ourselves, and we affirm to ourselves that we are enough.

It is the opposite of self-judgment, self-criticism, perfectionism and comparison. I prefer to think of this as experiencing a feeling of sweetness towards ourselves as if we were friends or small children. In reality, what it looks like means speaking and behaving kindly to ourselves, and we forgive ourselves when things go wrong.

2. Common humanity

Often we forget as human beings, we are imperfect and prone to making mistakes. We are all connected in our suffering, or as I like to say, we are all screwed up!

Focusing on the common humanity that connects us all rather than the differences that divide us makes us feel we are not alone and our struggles are universal. It then becomes easier to let go and accept ourselves and our situation as it is.

This self-love element gives us a broader perspective and allows us to be ourselves and feel okay because we are normal rather than feel like a loser or a freak. Then we are less likely to fall into the comparison trap where we compare our insides with other people's outsides and believe they 'have it all together.

3. Mindfulness

By paying attention to the here and now, we are more likely to catch ourselves when we fall victim to self-judgment and self-criticism and to take steps to bring in self-compassion to help restore the balance. Simultaneously, we don't ignore or exaggerate our suffering; we simply notice it as we move to comfort ourselves immediately.

This is especially valuable when things go wrong because of our negative reactions. After all, when things are fine, we are just cruising along in life. This looks like in reality because we can notice and validate our underlying feelings and needs and take time out to process them at the moment with lots of self-love and forgiveness, as opposed to dealing with them in hindsight not dealing with them at all.

As a recovering perfectionist, this is a topic close to my heart. I was very motivated to do more and be more, but the motivation came from a place of fear and scarcity – I'm not smart enough or What would other people think? – rather than a place of love and abundance, which has thoughts like I know enough and I'll be fine no matter what others think.

So even though I managed to be productive and achieve most of the goals I set for myself, I didn't feel any lasting joy and satisfaction with my achievements, and I was constantly striving for the next set of goals to 'improve' myself.

In other words, I kept moving my own goalposts. My to-do list was endless and constantly growing. Deep down, I felt there was something fundamentally wrong with me, and I needed to be fixed. It wasn't until I had a good grasp of self-love that I began to accept myself regardless of what I got done (or didn't).

And self-love came to my rescue again after my devastating breakup. Instead of beating myself up for and blaming the breakup on me, I decided I was worth my own love, and I cut myself a massive amount of slack. I took really good care of myself, stayed physically active, and had plenty of rest. And I gave myself permission to grieve and to cry whenever I felt like it instead of stuffing it all down.

Rebuilding Self-Worth

This is to do with the idea of self-worth or self-esteem, i.e., how we see or value ourselves. Sadly, many of us value ourselves poorly, and we see ourselves as less than or not enough. It's likely that our self-worth has been slowly eroded over time during a relationship and then took a huge hit with the breakup or divorce itself.

Our sense of inferiority or inadequacy means we find it hard to even like ourselves, let alone love. Given our happiness and sense of fulfillment are related to how much we love and accept ourselves, it's little wonder that we feel miserable and unfulfilled.

There are many reasons we have low self-worth, and one of the main ones is that we conflate our external circumstances or goals with our internal self-worth. We think, I'll be enough when I meet someone special / find my dream job / _____ (fill the blank). However, our circumstances and goals are mostly outside our control. It's fine when things are going well or when we achieve our goals, but when things don't go as expected, our self-worth inevitably suffers.

For example, our self-worth is usually at an all-time low when we've just experienced a breakup or divorce. And it's normal, and even the most confident amongst us will experience a slump in our self-worth.

Nonetheless, people who can separate the breakup from their self-worth are better at bouncing back afterward. They are also more likely to use the experience to help them thrive and choose their next relationship from a place of strength rather than just survive and settle for less.

By the way, nothing wrong with wanting more and better things in our lives. However, it becomes problematic when we depend on achieving our goals and other things to go our way to be happy, not realizing that a) we don't always achieve our goals or dreams, and b) it's nobody else's job to make us happy. They can only make our job easier, but it's still our job at the end of the day.

Self-love, on the other hand, is inside yourself and, therefore, within your control. It is not dependent on external circumstances, achievements or other people.

Once you learn how to love yourself unconditionally and see yourself as worthy of that love no matter what, your self-worth stays intact and remains constant.

Becoming the Person You Love

First, we need to start mentally untangling our self-worth from our external circumstances or goals. In other words, producing thoughts like my divorce sucks, but I don't suck, Or, just because I haven't achieved my goals, it doesn't mean I'm a loser. Indeed, it's essential to look at what you make your negative circumstances or your lack of achievements mean in terms of your self-worth. And it doesn't have to mean anything.

Indeed, you are already worthy. You were loved into being. And just as human, you come 'pre-approved! No further circumstances, actions or achievements are required.

Therefore, your goals are only for creating more happiness in your life, not to increase your own self-worth.

Many of us think getting our dream partner or our dream job will somehow make us more worthy, so we keep chasing after our next goal or striving to change our circumstances, putting our happiness on hold all the while. However, no amount of external validation will increase our self-worth in the long run; you may enjoy your achievements or praises from others for now, but soon you will be back on the hamster wheel hungry for more.

One of the biggest enemies to self-love as well as to self-worth is our inner critic. We have already discussed it in length in chapter five. (If you have skipped the chapter, it would be really useful to go back to find out how we can avoid being our worst enemy.)

For now, just remember that the way we talk to ourselves matters a great deal, and language is how we make sense of ourselves, others and the world. Unfortunately, our muscles for loving self-talk have likely atrophied from years of disuse, so we need to re-condition ourselves with positive, uplifting language in our inner dialogue.

Finally, unlike striving for external circumstances or achievements, every act of self-love and self-care improves our self-worth because it's a message to ourselves that what we need and want matters. Therefore we ourselves are important and worthy.

Common Barriers

If self-love and self-compassion are so vital, why aren't we all more self-loving and kinder towards ourselves daily? The simple answer is that many people are confused about self-compassion.

TAKING CARE OF YOURSELF

It's tough to admit, but sometimes there are things that we just can't figure out ourselves. So when you're going through a hard time, it's important to reach out and talk about what's going on. Talking about your feelings can help you better understand what you're feeling, like why it hurts so much. You might even discover some coping strategies that work for you that you weren't aware of before — such as journaling or meditating.

Without a doubt, hearing others' stories about how they dealt with heartbreak can be helpful. But sometimes, even talking about your feelings isn't enough. Sometimes you need some professional help to deal with the pain of being broken up with — whether it's just something to ease the passing of time or to get you back on your feet again.

When you're dating someone new, it can be hard to find a good balance between spending time alone and spending time with your new love interest. This is especially true when things are still brand new.

If you're going through a breakup, it can be hard to figure out how long to wait before contacting your ex. You might want to try sending them a text or leaving them a voice mail, and another option is giving the silent treatment.

While there isn't one rule that will apply to everyone, here is some general advice on how to deal with a breakup. Breakups are never easy, and sometimes the pain can last for years after you split up with someone you cared for deeply. It takes time to heal after any kind of loss, but if you know what signs to look out for, chances are your recovery will go much more smoothly.

1. Take your time.

It can be hard to accept that someone you cared about had moved on, especially if they said or did something to provoke you when they broke up with you. Try to give yourself some space to heal without feeling pressured by those around you. If someone is trying to guilt-trip you into getting back together, it's definitely time for a break-up and moves forward with a fresh start.

2. Look inward first, then outwardly

It can be easy to forget that we are responsible for our own happiness and feelings of self-worth, even when somebody else is the one who broke your heart or caused the breakup in the first place. Don't take any of it personally. How someone else feels about you is not your responsibility. If they are unhappy about something you did in the past, think about what it is that they might be jealous of. It may be something as simple as who you hang out with, or how much money you make, or maybe even your habits in bed.

3. Accept that things have to change

There comes a time when a relationship changes so drastically that you just have to accept it and move on with your life. This can be hard if you're still hung up on the breakup and can't let go of old feelings or lingering resentment towards your ex-partner.

4. Don't rush into a rebound relationship

A new relationship realizing is a quick fix to get over your last relationship and resume dating. You may think that it will comfort you in the beginning, but chances are, you won't actually be able to move on until you've dealt with your breakup properly. Give yourself some time to mourn the loss of what could have been with your ex-partner before attempting to heal by jumping right back in.

5. Know when to stay away

It can be difficult to make drastic changes because we feel like we're no longer over someone from our past, especially if they try contacting us or trying to rekindle things after several months of being broken up. You may also feel tempted to try again, especially when you're feeling emotional or vulnerable.

6. Take it slow

If you're feeling overwhelmed about the changes that have taken place in your life after the breakup, it's important to take things slow and deal with the pain in small manageable pieces. This will make the long-term recovery process easier.

7. Plan ahead

Having a plan for coping with a breakup can help ease some of your anxiety and stress levels after such a big change has taken place in your life. Having a plan of action will allow you to feel more prepared and confident when dealing with painful emotions that come up during the healing process.

8. Be patient

Coping with a breakup is not easy, but it usually takes anywhere from six weeks to three months for the pain to go away completely.

9. Communicate with others

If you're having trouble getting through your breakup, consider talking to somebody you trust who will be able to help you get through the rough patches. A good listener can be incredibly comforting when dealing with something like a breakup, especially if they've been through something similar and can give you some advice on how they coped in the past.

TAKING CARE OF YOUR KIDS

Taking care of yourself after a breakup isn't easy, but taking care of your children? It can be so much more difficult. If you're in this situation, don't worry. You are not alone.

It can be really difficult to take care of yourself after a breakup, but it's even harder when you have children. If you are in this situation, the best thing to do is remember that there are things that they might need during and after the divorce. So we created this post to help guide you through these trying times and provide some insight on what might be best for your kids so that they can stay happy and healthy while everything changes around them. We've included some comfort tips for your kids based on age, as well as advice on how to get back into being their parent again.

What happens to my kids after a breakup?

The divorce process can happen at any time. It can be anytime between the day you say the words "I don't love you anymore" and when your divorce is final. If this is the case, you will need to take care of your kids because they might still see their father and mother as a couple unless, of course, you've decided to adopt them or foster them. Instead of being with their natural parents, they will probably see their legal parents for regular visitation days. Or maybe they'll only see one parent every couple of months at the most. Either way, it's bound to be stressful for your children until things are settled in court.

How can I prepare my kids?

After those awful words, "I don't love you anymore," it's inevitable that your children will be affected. Usually, they are sad and confused, but they will soon start to get more curious about what's happening. They might ask questions that make you feel queasy answering them. These are normal reactions to the trauma of a divorce. You don't have to feel guilty about explaining things to them, but you do have to remember what information is appropriate for them to know and what isn't.

Your children will be confused because you and their father or mother are no longer together. They might feel sad, scared or angry about the things that are happening. Your main goal is to make them feel safe and loved at all times, even if your ex makes them feel otherwise. let them know that they can always come to you with questions and worries for as long as they need to. Explain to them why it's not working anymore, but try not to get into all of the details about how you or their dad/mom are feeling. You want your kids to know that you're taking care of everything differently now, but that doesn't mean you love them any less than before.

It's also a good idea to think ahead about how your children will handle everything if they have to move. It's best to give them a general idea of what they can expect, but don't tell them your plans ahead of time. For example, if you are taking them and their dad/mom in, explain that you will probably be renting somewhere for a while until you get on your feet again. Or that maybe it'll be just you and the kids.

How do I take care of myself?

Despite the emotions you're going through, your main focus should always be taking care of yourself. You cannot help yourself and your children if you're not doing what's best for YOU.

Remember to eat well and get plenty of sleep. Your body will feel exhausted and weak from all of this stress, but you have to do your best to take care of yourself. Remember, the very first thing you need to do is break up with your partner. You need time to heal, time to learn how to live without each other, and time for your children to heal as well.

Take a break from work for a while if possible so that you can focus on healing.

It's hard for many of us to accept that we can be happy without having to be with someone. Some people need someone to feel alive and feel like they cease to exist when they're alone. I can assure you that once you accept that you can be perfectly happy without someone, the other steps will seem much easier. For me, accepting that this was something I could do on my own saved me a lot of heartaches.

You won't be able to tell your children how to deal with heartbreak if you're caught up in it yourself. They need a rock to cling onto emotionally, and they need to know that they don't have to do it alone either. Giving them tools and confidence in themselves is what they need most.

Don't over-explain or overemphasize the relationship (even though this might feel good).

Whether you're talking to them or yourself, over-explaining the breakup will only make you look foolish. You'll be saying something that's "false," and when they hear it from you, they'll be thinking of the false version as the truth.

This is not your partner's fault, and your children won't blame them for what happened, but you want to minimize any pain your children might experience by telling them that you are not angry with them. Tell them that you understand how hard to be a child is, but they still need to take care of themselves while dealing with this. And if they don't, then let them go.

Set some time aside and make a list of the things you want to do or the things you want to buy. While there's nothing wrong with taking time for yourself, it's vital that you do accomplish some of those things on your list. Use this time as a way to be productive as well as take care of yourself.

Take care of your health in whatever way is best for you.

Exercise, meditation, eating well...these are all ways that we can take care of our own hearts, especially if we did not always do this while someone else was in our lives. Perhaps your heartbreak will motivate you to improve areas of your life that you might not have addressed before.

For some people, working out becomes essential after a heartbreak. It can help them clear their minds and burn off some of the excess energy they are feeling, especially if they didn't always get enough exercise before their breakup.

Meditation can do wonders for your emotional state and help you find clarity in situations where you might not have had it previously. There's a reason why most religions have some sort of meditation practice for people who want to get closer to God.

Eating well can be a way to help you heal and also make yourself feel better. Even if you normally don't care about how healthy your food is, there might be something about the heartbreak that makes you want to start taking better care of yourself.

There will be some people whose health takes a turn for the worse after a breakup. If this is the case for you, I highly recommend getting professional help.

Learn how to move on when it's time to move on.

One of the most important things that we all have to learn at some point in our lives is how to move on when something or someone precious has come and gone from our lives. That's what we call letting go.

When we feel like there's an opportunity for us to learn from our past experiences, letting go can be easier. If you're someone who needs or wants closure, make sure that you get it. Then let yourself move on and remember that life is not over.

Don't expect your children to do anything different than they have been doing, and remind them of what you want them to do.

You want your children to live well and find their own happiness while considering themselves first in most cases. Teach them how to respect themselves and others to live successful lives without compromising their morals or values.

CONCLUSION - THE PATH TO FIND TRUE LOVE

Many people often feel after going through a breakup that there is no point in finding love again. They may question if they will ever be in love again or find someone to make them happy. But the truth is that time heals all wounds, and with time you will be able to open your heart to someone new.

A broken heart is the most painful feeling you will ever go through. You may feel that you are losing the closest person to you and all of your relationship. This will prove to break your spirit but don't worry, as time will heal everything.

All it takes is a little time and patience, and you will soon be ready to love again. But of course, it's never easy, especially if it's your first love or if you have never had a relationship before. But once you keep an open mind about everything, there is no reason why you can't get back out there and find someone new and find real love again.

But first, I want to introduce you to the concept of 'disqualification' and help you understand that your past relationship should not stop you from finding a new one.

The concept of disqualification is about how your past relationship should not be a factor when it comes to finding new love. So basically, it's about either going through relationship history or whether you got dumped by someone else before. Because the truth is that everyone has been hurt in their life, but this doesn't mean that they will not find the one person who can make them happy again.

If you keep blaming your past relationship for your current situation, then it's only a matter of time before you give up on love and stop hoping for it to come back to you. Simply put, do not let the past prevent you from moving forward and finding a new partner. If there was something wrong with your partner in the past, then there is no way that this is still going on or that he will never be able to change his ways or that everything is still going well with him because he's changed.

If you are still blaming him for everything, then it's time to stop this and love again. So unless you want to be single forever, start putting yourself out there and find a new partner.

When we break up with someone, we may start comparing our new partner with the last one, but this should never be done because they will never be exactly the same. For example, if you compare your new partner's kind, don't forget that he is not responsible for what another man did to you in the past.

I have always believed that love comes in different ways, and not everyone has been lucky enough to find the person with whom they want to spend their life. But that's okay because you will find the one person who can make you happy in the future.

But in order to do so, there are a few things that you should keep in mind. First of all, you need to understand that time is your best friend to heal a broken heart. I mean by this that the longer you stay away from your ex-lover, the more time you will have to heal and get over this relationship.

Acknowledge the pain

When you went through a painful break-up, you may have wanted to forget it ever happened. It can be tempting to try and avoid thinking and talking about what happened. But if you want to move on, you have to acknowledge the pain that you are in. You will need to feel it, acknowledge it and express it. This is the first step towards healing your broken heart. You need to let yourself cry and get all of your emotions out; otherwise, they will just build up inside you until they eventually make everything worse.

Stop blaming yourself

Many people go through a breakup when they realize that things about themselves contributed to their situation. They may have been too clingy or too needy, and now they end up thinking that they are stupid and can't trust anyone. If you go through a break-up, thinking that you should've done something better will only leave you feeling worse. Just stop blaming yourself for anything that happened and move on with your life.

Think about the future

After being hurt by someone else, it can sometimes be tempting to take the path of least resistance. You may feel like you don't want to be in a relationship and just want to live your life alone. But later, you will realize that this isn't going to fix anything, and it is going to become harder as time goes by.

A person who isn't in a relationship will always think about being in a relationship and how much they would like to have one. But you are just going to be alone, not in a relationship and thinking about it constantly. Instead of taking the path of least resistance, you should think about your future. Think about what kind of person you want to meet. If the right person comes along, investing your time into that relationship will only make things better for you. But if you aren't putting any effort into finding the right person for you, then you will never find happiness.

This may sound like an obvious process, but it is important. If you want to find happiness again after a break-up, you have to be willing to move on with your life, and otherwise, nothing will ever get better for you.

Loving someone again after a heartbreak can be really difficult, but it will happen when the time is right. Just keep reminding yourself of that and never give up hope!

www.ingramcontent.com/pod-product-compliance
Lightning Source LLC
Chambersburg PA
CBHW071517080526
44588CB00011B/1453